Workstations and Local Area Networks for Librarians

Kieth Wright

American Library Association
Chicago and London 1990

The paper used in this publication meets the minimum requirements of American National Standard for Information Sciences—Permanence of Paper for Printed Library Materials, ANSI Z39.48-1984. ∞

Designed by Jeanne Wolfgeher and Omega Publishing Services, Inc.
Composed in Times Roman on
  Compugraphic 8600 by
  WordWorks, Inc.
Printed on 50-pound Glatfelter,
  a pH-neutral stock, and bound
  in 10-point Carolina cover stock
  by Braun-Brumfield, Inc.

Library of Congress Cataloging-in-Publication Data

Wright, Kieth C., 1933–
    Workstations and local area networks for librarians / Kieth Wright.
        p.   cm.
    Includes bibliographical references.
    ISBN 0-8389-0538-2 (alk. paper)
    1. Microcomputer workstations—Library applications. 2. Local area networks (Computer networks). 3. Communication in library administration. 4. Communication in library science. 5. Libraries—Automation. I. Title.
    Z678.93.M53W75   1990
    025.1′028546—dc20   90-489

Printed in the United States of America.

93 92 91 90   5 4 3 2 1

C O N T E N T S

INTRODUCTION 1

1. Workstations and Local Area Networks 3

2. Planning and Managing: The Human Factor 25

3. Workstation Applications 49

4. Public Access to Workstations and the Local Area Network 67

5. Technical Services Uses 85

6. Ergonomics and Library Operations 101

7. Protocols, Topologies, Processing, and Procedures 114

APPENDIXES

    A. Producers of Workstations 133

    B. Network Characteristics 135

    C. Local Area Network Manufacturers 139

BIBLIOGRAPHY 145

INDEX 149

richest hard-rock gold mining districts in the world.

Many of the people and events in this story, such as the Kidders, Miss Doom, the Ladies Relief Society, and Donation Day, are based on historical fact. Others are fictional characters who show the mixture of races and cultures that did once exist in Grass Valley and other early gold-mining communities.

In the last one hundred years, Grass Valley has changed. The little "Never Come, Never Go" railroad that once ran from Colfax through Grass Valley to Nevada City is gone. It stopped running in 1942 when the large gold mines were shut down during World War II. The train and mine whistles are silent. The stamp mills are silent.

Yet, the happy voices of children are loud and clear as they march on Donation Day each year in late December. Girls, like Thomasina, Allison, and Colleen, have marched in the parades for generations. Local newspapers never listed the names of the first girls to march.

Oh, and women can now vote.

On a still, starry night, I can sometimes hear the tap, tap, tap of Winny's little pick as she warns me to never let my child-like imagination be dimmed by too much adult-thinking.

I **always** heed her warning.

About the Author

This is the only fictional book that Juanita Kennedy Browne wrote for children. She had written hundreds of articles for newspapers and magazine and was the author of three books published by the Nevada County Historical Society, as well as three Nevada County Collector's Calendars published by the Sierra Nevada Memorial Hospital Foundation.

Until her death in an automobile accident on March 30, 1993, Juanita had been living on a Christmas tree farm in The Hollow in Grass Valley, California. Shortly before that tragic event, while preparing for publication of this book, Juanita explained why she had written this particular book. Speaking of herself in the third person, she wrote: "She thinks a lot about Christmas trees and Christmas tree decorations. One cold winter morning, a female Tommyknocker appeared in a Douglas fir tree and warned Juanita that before she grew too old she should write this book and ask her granddaughter Allison to illustrate it. They did as the Tommyknocker asked."

About the Artist

Allison Bridgman is Juanita Browne's 11-year-old granddaughter. Allison is in the sixth grade at the De Portola Middle School in San Diego, California. She likes to read. She also practices aikido and piano and has won awards in art, poetry, and spelling. Allison plans to be either a teacher or an author when she grows up.

About a Special Advisor

Joe Bridgman is Juanita Browne's 10-year-old grandson. He, too, lives in San Diego and is in the fourth grade at Tierrasanta Elementary School. Joe gave both Grandma Nita and Allison good advice on the book and illustrations. Joe has won awards in music and in the Balboa Park Essay Contest. Joe also practices aikido and piano. He plans to be either a policeman or a baseball player when he grows up.

References

Nuggets of Nevada County History, by Juanita Kennedy Browne. Nevada City, California: Nevada County Historical Society, 1983.

Files of *The Union* newspaper (Grass Valley, California).

Photo Credits

The photographs on pages 2, 5, 11, 13, 14, 18, 26–27, and 40 are reproduced here by courtesy of Heritage Graphics of Grass Valley, California. The photographs on pages 6, 37, and 41 are from the Alfred M. Kramm Collection and are reproduced by courtesy of Harriet Jakobs.

Introduction

The 1980s saw tremendous developments in the area of personal computers and related communication systems. The pace of change was staggering. FAX machines were introduced one year and became universal (even in your automobile) by the next year. One fast personal computer with large memory capacity was rapidly replaced by another one with even more memory capacity and at a lower cost. Institutions developed internal and external computer-based communication systems only to find those systems outdated by the pace of technological development.

This book grew out of a decade's experience with libraries and educational institutions as the staff of those institutions began to use microcomputers for specific library functions. Libraries utilize a wide range of computer-based communication systems and are now developing local area networks within institutions and wide area networks across the world. Often the technology of these systems is better understood than the reasons that libraries use them.

Knowing why the library needs to get into local area networking and workstations is of critical importance. Chapter 1 of this book provides some basic information on workstations and local area networks in the context of the goals and objectives of particular libraries. Once the goals and objectives of this involvement have been clarified, the planning process for defining network needs and implementing a local area network with workstations can begin. Chapter 2 focuses on planning and managing the local area network and the human side of the operation, including issues in designing and supervising workstation areas. Chapter 3 discusses library management uses of workstations and local area networks. Chapter 4 outlines the varied uses of these devices by the library's public. Chapter 5 presents technical services uses of workstations and local area networks in acquisitions and cataloging. Chapter 6 introduces essential human factors (ergonomics) in the selection and placement of workstations for use by the library staff and public. Chapter 7 describes how workstations operate in local area networks and reviews some of the standards and technical issues related to local area networks and workstations.

1

This book is written to help the librarian move from basic use of the personal computer into the use of workstations and local area networks. Libraries are now purchasing increasingly complex computer-based communication systems. Making that move is not simple, so various chapters raise critical issues and questions about specific applications, types of equipment and software, and the users of these more sophisticated systems. Suggestions for further reading are presented at the end of each chapter. References cited in each chapter are found in the bibliography at the end of the book.

1

Workstations and Local Area Networks

If (aircraft technology) had evolved as spectacularly as the computer industry over the last 25 years, a Boeing 767 would cost $500 today and it would circle the globe in 20 minutes on 5 gallons of fuel.
[Toong and Gupta, 1982, p. 87]

The two major forces moving librarians toward using personal computers have been: (1) the sharp reduction in the cost of computer systems, and (2) the dramatic increase in their capacity to do needed work. This chapter discusses personal computers, workstations, and communication between computers including local area networks as these systems can be used in libraries. Basic concepts and limitations of personal computers, workstations, and local area networks are presented.

Personal Computers and Libraries

As prices for computer equipment and software fell many librarians began to use personal computers. These personal computers had the ability to store about 64,000 typed characters (64K); application programs and information were stored on floppy disks; and printing was done on a nine-pin dot-matrix printer. Readers interested in the history of personal computers, their current uses, and possible future applications are referred to "Microcomputers in Libraries" by Wallace and Giglierano (1989). They agree with Pratt (1984) that the literature concerning personal computers in libraries is, "a mile wide and an inch deep." Even though the early machines were slow, had limited memory capacity, and the dot-matrix printing was crude, librarians discovered that word-processing programs, accounting spreadsheets, and simple databases used for bibliographies, patron lists, and the like could be easily created and updated using these computers. The ability to make easy revisions and to use the same information in different publications convinced many librarians to use personal computers in their daily work.

When the Tandy Corporation introduced the Model I personal computer for less than one thousand dollars many individuals bought machines. At the same time the Apple Corporation's Apple II was being introduced into school and library settings throughout the country. These machines increased the number of computers in the world by about 200,000 over a period of several years. When IBM corporation introduced their "PC" machine and it was adopted by the business community, the future of the personal computer as a regular part of the operation of most organizations was assured.

Other librarians began their experience with personal computers when various online systems started to replace the former terminal connections with personal computers and modems (modulator-demodulators which convert the computer signals to telephone signals or vice versa). Software programs allowed the personal computer to control the modem, access remote databases, and store the information received from the remote computer. Systems like the National Library of Medicine and the Ohio College Library Center (now Online Computer Library Center) worked hard to make the connections between the local library terminal and the larger computer as easy as possible. The rules for signing on to the systems and the commands for using the systems were regularized either by the original vendors or by other vendors such as DIALOG and BRS. Many librarians participated in wide area information networks without a great deal of difficulty. Often they did not realize the telecommunications possibilities or problems of these systems.

During this time personal computers were used as stand-alone systems that could handle one application at a time. Software was developed with this one-at-a-time application in mind. Individuals using the personal computer selected the appropriate application program (such as word processing), inserted the floppy disk in the disk drive, placed a formatted data disk in the second drive, and started the computer. Typically the program disk contained startup instructions for the computer so that the first screen the user saw was the introductory screen for the particular program. An individual who wanted to switch programs inserted the disk for that program and restarted the computer.

Each applications program and its associated data disks could be kept together. The capability to relate management applications to technical services and online reference services being done in other parts of the building only became clear when personal computers began to be used as terminals accessing cataloging data (OCLC or RLIN) or for online reference services (DIALOG, SDC, or BRS). Early users of personal computers faced a major problem: information stored on one brand of computer could not be read by another brand of computer, even though the disks seemed to be identical. Different companies created different ways to electrically format their floppy disks. Some individuals got around this problem by connecting two different brands of computers through the telephone system using a modem. With a modem, people can use two computers, the telephone, and communications software to send and receive files across telephone lines.

Many modems translate the direct current signals from a computer into analog signals sent over telephone lines. Some modems handle radio frequencies and light signals. Modem speed for remote access via telephone has increased over the last few years so that what was once sent at thirty characters (300 baud) a second can now be sent at much higher speeds. Anyone who has used The Source, Compuserve, DIALOG or other online systems has experienced one of the forms of networking.

Modem speeds have increased dramatically during the 1980s. Top speeds of 1,200 bits per second (bps) were typical in the 1970s. Operating speeds have climbed to 2,400, 4,800, and 9,600 bps. Leased-line telephone service can supply from 9,600 bps up to 19,200 bps utilizing more complex hardware systems. Much of the demand for these high speed systems comes from the business world—particularly the banking industry which uses the systems for the electronic transfer of money. As the speed of modems has increased, the cost of increased speed has gone down.

Another change on the modem scene has been the increased ability to write a "script" for the interactions with a host computer. For example, the SCOPE program in Smartcom III allows the user to write a program which will contact a remote computer at specified time intervals and download selected information into a file. On some computers this program can run in the background while the operator is running another program. Other programs allow operation of the modem and remote computer from *within* application programs so that while a user is working with a spreadsheet or database program, he or she can contact a remote computer and load information in the applications program in appropriate format for that application. DIALOG services now offer some database information which can be automatically downloaded into database and spreadsheet formats.

Although the transmission of data at 30 to 240 characters per second is slow, many people use such networks to exchange information. For example, loading 16,000 bytes of information at 30 characters per second takes about nine minutes. Loading the same information from a floppy disk takes one second (or less).

When only text files are involved (and not special control characters as in popular word-processing programs) easy transfers of text can be made between many different types of computers. Both computers must have some type of communications software that allows for sending and receiving text messages and saving the text received. Most word-processing programs make the capacity to save files as text on a disk, and most personal computers save the text in ASCII code so that the text can be manipulated on the receiving end.

When two computers are connected directly by cable through the serial ports, a modem eliminator is often used. This wiring device use connects two personal computers without modems. It is sometimes called a "null modem." Such devices are limited in the distance over which transmissions can be sent (usually about 1,000 feet). Using appropriate communications software for each computer and connecting the pins of the serial ports of the two personal computers in appropriate ways, the users can share files between the two machines.

As individuals began to store larger and larger amounts of data, larger storage devices became necessary. Users of personal computers began to buy hard-disk drives which store the same amount of information as hundreds of floppy disks. These drives allow for the storage of large amounts of data without repeatedly changing floppy disks. Another advantage of the hard disks is that the hard disk can be divided into subdirectories so that different programs and their related data can be stored on the same hard disk. Subdirectories allow the personal computer user to "multitask" the computer without switching floppy disks in and out of disk drives. The user simply ends one program and initiates another by moving from one subdirectory of the hard disk to another and issuing the appropriate commands. Data for programs can be stored in different subdirectories or on floppy disks. Such multitasking is not "coprocessing" as now defined in the computer industry. Coprocessing allows several application programs to run at the same time, so that changes made by one program will be reflected in the data of several programs.

A number of companies began to offer menu programs which allow the user to set up programs and data files in subdirectories and move from one to another by means of selecting a number on the menu. Such menu programs (or batch files in IBM-type machines) not only allow for the initiation of programs, but also return the user to the menu when a program is ended. Menu-driven programs became especially popular in situations where staff members did not have a great deal of personal-computer experience and the number of possible applications programs was limited. A typical menu is shown in Figure 1.

Equipment costs have gone down significantly as the computing power and storage capacity of personal computer systems has increased enormously. If computing capacity (central processing capacity, memory capacity, and disk storage capacity) is held constant, costs have declined dramat-

Figure 1.
A Typical Menu

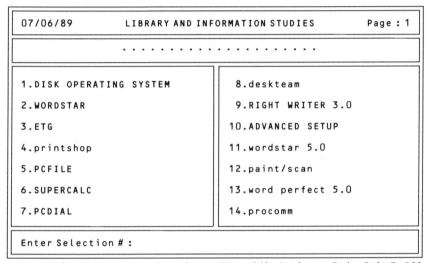

```
PLEASE SELECT ONE OF THE FOLLOWING:

(1) USE WORDSTAR 4.0

(2) USE PC-FILE

(3) USE SUPERCALC 4.0

(4) USE PROGRAMS IN THE DISK SYSTEM SUBFILE

(5) TERMINATE PROCESSING

SELECT 1,2,3,4 OR 5
```

```
07/06/89          LIBRARY AND INFORMATION STUDIES          Page : 1

              . . . . . . . . . . . . . . . . . . .

1.DISK OPERATING SYSTEM            8.deskteam

2.WORDSTAR                         9.RIGHT WRITER 3.0

3.ETG                              10.ADVANCED SETUP

4.printshop                        11.wordstar 5.0

5.PCFILE                           12.paint/scan

6.SUPERCALC                        13.word perfect 5.0

7.PCDIAL                           14.procomm

Enter Selection # :

Pg Up = Prior Page   Pg Dn = Next Page   Ins = Edit Options   End = Exit To DOS
```

ically. Anderla and Dunning (1987) have estimated that computer costs will continue to decline at about 25 percent per year (without adjustment for inflation). The user of a personal computer in 1990 can have the same power for computing as the user of the IBM 370 in 1975. In addition, the current desktop personal computer operates much faster than the earlier machines because of improved CPU microchips. In 1990 it is possible for the personal-computer user to assemble a machine that has far greater capacity in computing speed, memory, and storage than many previous mainframe computers—at much lower cost. For instance, in 1975 one could purchase an IBM 370 for $500,000 to $1 million; in 1980 one could buy a DEC VAX for $225,000; and by 1990 an 80386 PC, comparable in capability, was available for only $6,000.

One example of reduced costs and increased capacities is the personal computer I used to create this book, which has more computing capacity and on-board memory than the IBM 360-75 used in 1975. In addition, the disk storage capacity of the machine has been increased to over 40 megabytes. I created the first programs I wrote on punch cards and submitted them to the operator of the IBM 360-75 at Columbia University. Debugging these programs and using them to process text from computer tapes for a language study of the use of English by educators was extremely time-consuming, not only for me but for the operating system of the computer. My current personal computer cost less than $2,000. Newer disk operating systems (OS/2 or Dos 4.01) would allow me to expand the internal memory (ROM) and the disk memory of my personal computer as far as necessary.

Large computers manipulate data files and do calculations very effectively, but doing word-processing formatting in real time slows down the big machine. The large computer is designed to take large amounts of data, manipulate them extensively, and produce the results in usable form. Interactions with a person at a terminal interrupt this process. With the personal computer, a person often takes up to one-half the cycles of the machine with specific instructions about format, fonts, and files. This difference means that word processing is very wasteful on a large computer but efficient on a personal computer, because the personal computer typically is doing only that one job at a time.

From Personal Computers to Workstations

The first stage in the development of the personal computer as workstation begins as librarians begin to add the ability to do more and more work on personal computers. The ability to do more work means faster processing speeds, more memory, more disk storage, more types of input and output: laser printers, image scanning devices, graphics capabilities. Such workstations process information more rapidly and make use of hard-disk storage capacities.

The second stage of workstation development begins when the workstations are connected to the "outside world" so that the user of the workstation can make use of online services, search a library catalog, or use files from another workstation or personal computer. These telephone-system–based connections allow librarians access to vast files of information produced by commercial firms, professional societies, and government agencies. Many librarians use networks for the first time in this second stage. At this stage, the user of the personal computer does not affect the contents of the files available on other computers. The user has access to but not manipulating control of the files. A variety of security systems (including passwords) are installed to ensure that such manipulation does not happen.

The third stage begins when workstations are connected in a local area network so that information can be created, modified, and communicated among workstations. For example, the staff wants to do cooperative reviewing of data, sharing of information for planning, writing of papers together, or sharing of expensive printers or plotters. Before local area networks such sharing usually meant making a copy of data on a floppy disk and giving it to the other party so they could view and manipulate that data on their personal computer—if their personal computer and disk operating system matched that of the original machine. In more recent times, the difference in disk format (even among PC-type computers) has made such sharing more difficult. Disk-drive formats now include: 360K, 1.2 megabytes, in 5¼-inch drives and 80 MK or 1.4 MK in 3½-inch drives.

Local area network software is designed to allow file sharing among all users on the network. This file sharing includes the ability to manipulate file contents. Many commercial workstations offer high-resolution graphics, "window" interfacing, large amounts (two to four megabytes) of memory, and large hard-disk capacities. A major reason for acquisition of a workstation-based local area network system is the need for multiple, concurrent access to large database files by several users at different sites in a building or local area. So-called workstations can be confused easily with the connecting PC-type computers through a cabling system. More powerful PC equipment and storage devices increasingly are making the distinction difficult to see. A listing of some of the current workstations available appears in appendix A at the end of this book.

The advantages of local area networks over "walking a disk" from one machine to another include:

the ability to share information without having to convert from one disk format to another. Computers with different size and capacity disk drives can communicate

the ability to share data in real time. There is no waiting "while I make a disk copy for you."

the ability to limit the size and cost of workstations connected to the network. Many local area networks have one workstation managing the LAN, holding files and connected to printers and other devices. Such workstations are called "file servers." In such situations, diskless workstations do not have to have disk drives but simply use the disk drive of the file server.

the ability to share expensive laser printers, plotters, and projection devices among a number of computers. In a LAN system, several workstations can share output and display devices without conflict. For example, printing tasks are queued by the file server and sent to the printer (or other device) when that device is free. The person using a workstation does not have to wait for printing to be completed before moving on to another task.

When two or more workstations are connected together electronically so that data can be shared, a local area network has been created. The problem of getting personal computers to work together in a system has been called "connectivity." Taking on a connection project between personal computers can be as simple as making an administrative decision on personal computer-software that sets a policy of utilizing one word-processing package, one database-management system, and one spreadsheet or integrated-software package. Kemper (1988, p. 187) defines a LAN as "a privately owned, user-administered communications facility extended over a limited geographic area." The differences between a local area network and more traditional communications networks are listed in Figure 2.

A typical local area network is a combination of several tools:

the network operating system software that controls the communication between computers
the network hardware made up of boards and cables
the computers that are connected

Figure 2.
Local Area Networks Contrasted with Traditional Telecommunications Systems

(1) Geographic area. Local area networks are *local.* Usually they are designed to serve an office area or a building.

(2) Ownership. The local library makes the system, operates it, fixes what breaks, and pays the bills. One cannot "pass the buck" to some outside vendor, unless there is a maintenance contract.

(3) Communications system. The LAN operates over cables supplied by the library, not one of the telecommunications companies. Selecting and installing cables is the library's responsibility.

the applications programs, which must be able to operate in concert with
the network operating system
the printers, plotters, fax machines attached to the system

Local area network systems come in several types, depending on the communications rules adopted by the manufacturer. These rules (or protocols) allow for an accepted set of communications procedures to be used throughout the system so data can be successfully transferred between computers across the cabling and to printers and other peripherals. Applications programs now used on personal computers such as word processing, spreadsheets, and database programs have network versions so that staff often does not have to learn a new program. The fact that network versions exist does not mean that the library staff will be able to use the current "stand-alone" version of software on the network; rather, the library may have to purchase a network version for use. Workstation-based local area networks come in various types; the next section will consider those types.

Types of Local Area Networks

Local area networks range from very simple to highly complex. Very simple local area networks are possible where a library has a common software policy combined with a policy on buying and maintaining only one type of personal computer and operating system. Such policies make connecting several personal computers as simple as acquiring a connecting cable and software packages that allow files to be sent from one personal computer to another.

Many offices have developed switching systems that allow several microcomputers to share one (or several) printers. Some of these systems are simply mechanical switches that allow the printer to be connected to a particular machine. Other print switchers contain "buffers" so data can be stored by connected microcomputers and sent (one at a time) to the selected printer. Still other systems are electronic and allow program control over what peripheral device is selected. The serial port on the back of a personal computer can be attached to such switching devices. Switch systems come in a variety of configurations which allow several persons to share one device, or one person to have selective access to several devices. With cross-matrix switching devices, two people can share two devices.

These peripheral sharing devices have direct competition from companies which offer low-cost peripheral sharing and some local area network capabilities. They are called, "software-based LANs," "serial-port LANs," or "zero-slot LANs." Whatever the name, they all function without special hardware, dedicated file servers or expensive cabling. Prices vary from about eighty dollars to three hundred dollars per microcomputer attached to other microcomputers (up to about twenty machines). Table 1 lists some of these local area networks.

In departments where high file capacity and fast communications speed are not necessary, these network systems allow for low-cost local area networking. Another advantage of these systems is their simplicity. They are operated from a menu-driven program and the connections usually consist of attaching twisted-wire pairs to the serial ports of the computer through an adaptive device. Having made the right connection and used an installation program, the user can start the system and begin to swap files, share printers and other devices. Some of the systems have an electronic message system allowing "mail" to be left for other users of the network system. When an individual starts his or her machine, a message is displayed about "mail waiting."

In these systems, each microcomputer in the system has software that can operate the system stored in memory. Examples of this style of operation include: Netline, Inc., Applied Knowledge Groups, Inc., *ZeroLAN* and *ZeroNet* software. Other suppliers make use of a central microcomputer to which all the other microcomputers must be attached. Such a computer is called a "file server." This file server controls network operations and is often dedicated to this task alone. Several network systems require such a file server, including: Novell *Netware*, Banyan Systems' *Vines*, and Univation's *Lifenet*. Other systems spread the file-server operations among the various connected computers (10Net Communication's *10Net*, Western Digital's *ViaNet*). In some situations, a file server with no keyboard will be used exclusively for network management and file storage. In other situations, that central microcomputer can be used as a workstation in the network but must also control all file and peripheral use. If users of the network are to use specific peripherals, those devices must be attached to the central microcomputer. Examples of this type include: Server Technology's *EasyPrint* and *EasyLAN*, as well as The Software Link's *LANLink/5X*.

If the security of data files is critical, simple networks isolated from the rest of the computers in the institution can be very effective. Since such systems are not physically connected with the rest of the system, there is no easy way for anyone to pry into these files. In other situations, such simple networks can be a subsystem of a larger local system allowing individuals to utilize the larger system as it is needed.

This latter arrangement has a number of advantages:

(1) Reducing the communication demand on the larger system

Since work groups communicate among themselves first and use the connection to other parts of the system less often, the main network

Table 1.
Local Area Networks

Product	Company	Number of Users	Local Attach?	Two-way File Transfer	Print Spool?	Speed (bps)	Type of Cable (Length)	Type of Network	Memory for Network	Command Drive	Background Operation	Security System	Price
ZeroLAN	Applied Knowledge	6	yes	yes	yes	115,200	RJ11 (1000)	any but closed ring	48K	DOS	yes	drive-locking	$150 per node
ZeroNet	Applied Knowledge	10	yes	yes	yes	115,200	RJ11 (1000)	any but closed ring	48K	DOS	yes	disk-locking read-only access	$300 per node
ManyLink	Netline	2	yes	yes	yes	19.2K	shielded (25)	chain or ring	40K	DOS or menu	yes	directory lock-file encrypting	$165
ManyLink for Workstations		8	yes	yes	yes	19.2K (25)	shielded ring (25)	chain or ring	40K	DOS or menu	yes	directory lock-file encrypting	$395
EasyLAN	Server Technology	14	no	yes	yes	56,000	unshield (50)	star or PBX	20K	DOS	yes	password file-lock	$220 (2) $120 per node
EasyPrint		8	no	no	yes	56,000	unshield (50)	star	20K	DOS or menu	yes		$120 (2)
LANLink/5X	The Software Link	17	no	yes	yes	575K	serial, null modem proprietary parallel (50)	star or ring	26K per node 32K for server	via batch file	yes		$275 parallel $175 serial $195 OS
DeskLink	Traveling Software	2	yes	yes	no	115,200	RJ11 (100)	ring	30K per node 128K for server	DOS or menu	no	file-lock	$140
LapLink Plus		2	yes	yes	no	115,200	shielded (100)	ring	30K per node 128K for server	DOS or menu	no	file-lock	$140
Brooklyn Bridge	White Crane Systems	2	yes	yes	no	115,200	null modem (8)		5K for server	DOS or menu	yes		$140

communication does not have to deal with data or electronic mail that is *within* the work group. Brownrigg (1985) estimates that 80 percent of the work done in a local area network will be at the local work-group level. As an example, few academic computer centers worry about word-processing file communications because most users of the system use their microcomputers to deal with word processing and other "local" applications.

(2) Enhancing peer-to-peer network efficiency

Most of these networks involve only a few microcomputer stations, so that the network operations are not degraded by the addition of too many stations. In the same way, the larger system does not have to "attend" these microcomputers on a full time basis.

(3) Simplifying the command structure of the network

These smaller networking systems have simple, menu-driven operating systems with a limited range of choices so that the staff members who use them find it easy to acquire the necessary skills to operate the network successfully.

(4) Reducing administrative supervision for the peer-to-peer network

Many of the low-end network systems do not require a great deal of administrative time. Policies and procedures must be implemented, and someone must be responsible for breakdowns and backups, but the administrative costs are not nearly as great as those in the high-end networks.

Cabling costs are held to a minimum because most systems utilize the twisted wire system or even wires now unused in the telephone system (usually the black and yellow wires—but have someone test first). Many larger local area networks require wiring with coaxial cable which is bulky and expensive. The low-end network systems may use wiring already in the walls of the institution and the standard PC serial ports for communication.

Naturally such systems are slow (especially those using the serial ports). Serial-port systems have a top data transfer speed of about 115,000 bits per second. However, many serial ports are not even designed for that speed. A speed ten times as great is required for many shared applications programs, shared database systems, and systems in which many files are moving between computers at (apparently) the same time. In the business world, local area networks have been developed to allow the largest number of people to share information at the least possible cost. Businesses have found several benefits arising from the use of local area networks: (1) provision of better, faster information for executive decision making, (2) holding down the cost of office operations, (3) increasing clerical level productivity, and (4) improving the communication flow in the operation.

The Workstation

The library field has seen rapid development in the use of personal computers as stand-alone tools for library management and for accessing large database files at remote computer facilities. Libraries are connected via telephone modems and FAX machines for communicating interlibrary-loan requests, document delivery, and electronic mail. Many libraries now have several personal computers used for management, patron access to information, interlibrary loan, acquisitions, and technical services. Large libraries and library systems have public access online catalogs which provide patron access to the holdings of the library, circulation control, technical services, bibliographic access, and database building. These larger systems often provide a variety of management access points for collection management, work flow studies, and budget management and planning.

Many library managers will find that large workstation-based networks have capacities beyond the library's immediate and anticipated needs. If the major network functions are peripheral sharing (printer, plotter, Laser printer) and file transfer, low-cost networking systems can provide these services for several microcomputers. Such networks are particularly effective in work-group settings where several people are involved in the same area of library work.

Librarians have been evaluating "scholar workstations." Alberico (1988) discusses the scholar's workstation, which would provide personal information retrieval capabilities. He notes that the current design is too expensive for most individuals or libraries, and suggests personal computer-based "reference/retrieval workstations" as a viable alternative. The fall 1988 introduction of the NeXT computer by Steven Jobs has been evaluated as a possible library workstation for the 1990s by Valauskas (1988, 1989). He describes the architecture of the three microprocessors in the NeXT machine, the vast memory possibilities, and the *NeXTStep* interface. Valauskas notes that any library workstation used by patrons and staff must have: (1) sufficient internal storage to deal with very large databases, and (2) the ability to connect easily to other workstations and mainframe computers. The NeXT machine clearly has massive optical-disk storage which is accessible (if slow).

The NeXT workstation has several features that make it an attractive alternative as a library workstation. These include: (1) the *Digital Librarian*—a utility for indexing, searching, and retrieving text, graphics, or sound. Valauskas tested the retrieval feature using very large optical-disk databases and found the speed and graphics capabilities outstanding. (2) the Sybase *SQL Database Server*—a powerful relational database package with networking capabilities. He believes the NeXT computer has the potential to introduce a new era in library workstations and transform the way typical library bibliographic data is manipulated by library staff and patrons.

The librarian's workstation will probably differ significantly from the proposed scholar's workstations. Librarians are in the business of supplying information in appropriate formats to a variety of client groups. They are rarely in the business of writing or illustrating for research, publication, or instruction in higher education. The basic function of the librarian's workstation, in a stand-alone environment or as part of a local area network, will continue to be finding, retrieving, and delivering information to meet the requests of clients.

High-priority items in the librarian's workstation will be:

capacity for high-quality, high-speed communication for the retrieval of information from remote databases, coupled with the ability to save that information for later distribution

capacity to reformat information into a variety of formats usable by various client groups: large print, audio output, Braille output, in digital form

capacity to deal with graphic images such as trademarks or chemical compound structures

capacity to do some desktop publishing in terms of selecting varied fonts and sizes of type in importing graphic images (from disk or scanning device) into documents for publication of brochures, bibliographies, and client information packages

capacity to connect as a node on a local area network with a variety of hardware attached (IBM, Macintosh) and a variety of applications programs

capacity to tap into local ongoing computer-based library operations for management analysis studies for work flow, costs, and modeling of alternatives

Another way to understand the librarian's workstation is to look at each of the components of that workstation: text display, graphics, printing, and operating speed.

Text Display

If the library is going to produce a great deal of such printed text as bibliographies or annual reports, and graphic enhancements are not a consideration, then the library will want to consider purchasing a monitor that allows for a full-page display in legible type. Currently, the author can display up to forty-five lines of text one hundred columns wide, but the size of the type requires extra concentration. Special preview features on some word-processing packages allow for reduced size displays of several pages, but the text and graphics are displayed in very small size. Currently available "thumbnail" size displays of multiple pages are of dubious value in any situation. Display cards and monitors are available that allow display of a full page of sixty-six lines eighty columns wide; however the current price is about nine hundred dollars.

When the library managers are using spreadsheet applications, they should consider software and display monitors that will allow a larger spreadsheet window on the screen. A typical screen setup will display eighty columns and about twenty rows of information. Some software can be used to reduce the size of the characters displayed and present a much larger window. Another option is an enhanced graphic monitor (or VGA monitor) which can display the larger window.

Graphics

If the printed materials need enhanced fonts of type and graphics, and the user wants to see what the page looks like before printing, "What You See is What You Get" (WYSIWYG) systems are to be preferred. Seeing the final product on the screen is preferable to making numerous laser-printer copies in an attempt to finalize the format. The library management will want to consider hardware and software that allow for the screen display of various type fonts and sizes as well as graphics. In libraries where many graphics mixed with text will be used in promotional materials, reports, and other publications, some type of digitizer for graphics may be required. The current crop of hand-held digitizers works, but real graphics production will require a scanner that can digitize a full page at a time. These machines cost between one and two thousand dollars, and many also offer the capacity to scan text into a word processor file through optical character-recognition software.

The Macintosh computer, with its mouse and desktop publishing software, has become very popular in situations where enhanced text and graphic capabilities are needed. The ability to design and produce high-quality brochures, bookmarks, and posters needs to be considered. Nordgren (1988) summarizes some of the advantages of the Macintosh configuration for library applications:

user-friendliness—icon-based commands controlled by a mouse type pointing device

innovative software—easy to use and unique in the ways that information can be organized to meet user needs (*Hypercard*)

versatility—integration of graphics, sound, text for desktop publishing, and public-information repackaging connectivity—easy connection to other Macs, Apples, and other networks through *Localtalk*, *Appletalk*, or *AppleFax*.

productivity—increased work output because of ease of training and use

reliability—Macs have an excellent reliability record

He goes on to discuss the limitations of the Macintosh in the library environment. These limitations related to the lack of software developed for specific materials handling functions (ordering, circulation, cataloging). There is also a lack of convenient interfaces for connection with large bibliographic utilities such as OCLC and RLN. Saffady (1987) gives a detailed report on the available software and hardware for the Macintosh. Readers of his report should be aware Apple has introduced even more software and connectivity possibilities in the last year.

Vandergrift (1988) explores some of the implications of the Macintosh-based *HyperCard* software for the users of personal computers. She argues that hypermedia (of which *HyperCard* is an example) allows the creators and the users of programs to explore information in new ways with a variety of media. *HyperCard* allows for the running of programs, peripherals, and a variety of other media (TV, CD-ROM, videodisks) with the push of a button. A wide variety of information formats can be incorporated into a package. The *HyperCard* buttons do need to be programmed by the creator or end user, but the possibilities are powerful. This hypermedia software will ultimately lead to enriched presentation of information in library management as well as education and business. Vandergrift also points out that the ease with which a variety of media formats can be joined inevitably brings up questions about the use (or abuse) of copyrighted materials in various forms. Further readings on hypertext applications will be found at the end of this chapter.

Similar icon-based, pointer-oriented graphic capabilities and hypermedia-type software are becoming more widely available for IBM-type machines. For example, *WordPerfect 5.0* has considerable font and graphics capabilities, and *WordStar 5.0* has a program capacity to deal with graphics. Low-resolution graphic designs can be created with *ETG* (*Easy Text and Graphics*), graphics software operating on an 80286 machine which allows a mouse-type operation of the graphic generator onto an EGA monitor in sixteen colors.

If graphics capabilities are essential for management functions, the staff should explore those text processors that treat all information as a graphic form (rather than text being treated as ASCII code). Before the purchase of any desktop-publishing equipment or software, it should be used by the staff. Paying for a training session at a community college or commercial firm is preferable to purchasing graphic-capacity equipment and software and then finding that it is very difficult to use.

Printing

When printing at the librarian's workstation is considered, the library staff should carefully analyze the actual uses of text materials in the library environment. Library management creates an amazing volume of text that does not require any special fonts, graphics, or layouts. The staff will become extremely frustrated with highly technical desktop-publishing layout systems if the bulk of their work is normal text output. Indeed, several consultants on *WordPerfect 5.0* recommend that the users set the system to measure pages in *WordPerfect 4.3* units of measure (that is columns and rows) for most purposes, rather than the more complex measurements in inches or points of type. If the library staff has access to software and dot-matrix or laser printers that can take character-oriented text and create different text sizes and fonts, the need for special desktop-publishing software is greatly reduced.

Along with the quality and type of textual materials that will be processed, the library staff needs to consider how that text will be made into hard copy. Printers abound in a variety of dot-matrix, daisywheel and laser forms. There is no question that the two thousand dollar laser printer (often enhanced with special font cartridges) produces excellent quality type that can be reproduced with professional level results. Still, sending memorandums, inventory lists, and drafts by laser printer seems excessively costly and very slow. In larger operations, the library is likely to tie one very good laser printer into a local area network and establish several sites where draft-quality printout can be produced at high speed with dot-matrix equipment.

Storage

Any library management workstation which has more than one dedicated use should have a hard-disk drive. Managing several different applications becomes much simpler, and most users can select what they want to do from a menu program. Chapter 1 has illustrations of two such menu programs. As the cost of hard-disk systems has fallen and disk operating systems have been developing that will handle more than thirty megabytes of disk space, many companies offer workstations with more memory. The general rule is: buy as much hard-disk capacity as you can afford, even if you do not think you will use it now.

Since hard-disk drives spin on bearings, the staff should expect that sometime in the future the drive will "crash" or the low level formatting of the disk will degrade, making access to files impossible. The library will need to keep backup copies of all applications software mounted on the hard disk and teach the users to keep particular data files on floppy disks. Even the floppy disks should have backup copies stored in another location if the data is significant for use at a later time.

If the library is storing a large number of programs and data on the hard disk, it is wise to invest in some kind of tape backup system which automatically backs up the disk files to a tape or tape-cartridge system. In local area network systems such a tape backup system may be part of the overall system so that the large files and programs stored on the file-server disk do not become inaccessible or lost.

Operating Speed

As librarians begin to use hard disks with multiple programs, the speed of the computer becomes significant. The more programs available, the more switching around is done. Loading files and bringing up applications takes time. The 80286 and the even-faster 80386 CPU chips make these activities easier to tolerate. Higher-speed chips are also used in newer Macintosh machines. When users are first introduced to a computer application, they are always impressed with its speed. After only a few weeks, they will want files to load faster, file saving to be executed more rapidly, and the general operation of the computer to be quicker. How soon we become impatient! When the library staff is found waiting for the computer, rather than the computer waiting for the staff, an upgrade in processing speed may be indicated.

Potential Network Problems

The process of moving from single personal-computer use to workstations connected to one another in a local area network can be difficult. Many times libraries (and other agencies) have acquired specific personal-computer hardware and software to do specific jobs. Personal computers are not always of the same type, and software is often not designed to be shared among different machines.

For example, in one library I know, microcomputing started as a public-access function when most of the area schools had Apple computers and software. The logical configuration was a group of Apple II computers and related applications software including *Appleworks*, a word processer, *Visicalc*, and some learning programs and games. Later the administrative office acquired a PC-type machine for word processing and eventually spreadsheet applications. As administrative word processing became the way to go, departments acquired various models of PC clones, word-processing packages available as "shareware" from ads in computing magazines. Now, interest in desktop publishing has caused the library to acquire a Macintosh with a laser printer and software for designing page layouts. Within a three-year period, the library has acquired three types of computers and about six types of word-processing software.

A typical barrier to local area networks in libraries is created by the equipment currently owned by the library. The question comes up, "What shall we do with the personal computer equipment (and software) that we now own?" Sometimes that equipment can become part of the network and sometimes the software can be used on a local area network. Used computer equipment and software are of little resale value. A big problem for the library administrator is owning several brands of personal computers that are not compatible.

Some local area network systems and software will allow the connection of different types of machines (which are often sub-networked by type). Such systems allow for the transfer of information between personal computers, but the applications software (like word processing) must be used at the local machine. Information can be exchanged, but it requires reformatting for use in the new environment. The more different types of personal computers and software, the greater the cost of connecting systems and replacing software and hardware.

Personal computers, workstations, and local area networks are often seen as "capital expenditures" rather than as "consumables." When the machine (or the system) is seen as a capital investment, libraries and schools typically think such investments will run forever (witness 16mm projectors in schools). Granted, equipment will need maintenance and parts replacement, but it should last ten to fifteen years. Any type of library computer installation should not be considered a long-term "capital item." Changes in the capacities of equipment and the requirements of the users will require at least updating and probably replacement every four to five years. It is possible to use outdated equipment and software.

I used a Sol Processor Technologies personal computer and word-processing software well into the 1980s, but I paid a price for that use in terms of slow processing speed, lots of disk swapping, and finally the breakdown of the system—with incredible loss of information on floppy disks that could not be run on any other machine. Every library will eventually need to replace and upgrade workstation equipment. When such times come, the library administrator has the opportunity to consider linking the new equipment into local area networks through appropriate purchases.

Many of the issues related to how library staff will react to workstations and local area networks will be explored in detail in chapter 2 of this book—Planning and Managing: The Human Factor. Not every library needs a local area network. Librarians should analyze the information-processing needs of the library as a system. It may be that the library has several systems of information processing that can operate as separate units providing necessary information for management planning and budget control. The style of management and staff or governing agencies may require specific types of information in specific formats which may create networking problems.

Considerations for moving from stand-alone personal computer operations to some form of network of computers include the following.

(1) The disk operating system:

Is the library using one of the DOS operating systems or are various departments using a variety of personal computers? Libraries using one system will be easier to network together.

(2) Speed of library operations:

Is the library seeking to speed up library operations? If increased data-transmission speed is a critical factor for large amounts of data, then the library will need a more complex and expensive LAN. If the library is moving from paper copies to electronic data communication for the first time, the low-cost systems will suffice. There is big difference between a system of electronic mail where short memos are being shared and a system that requires transferring large files of text or spreadsheet numbers and formulas.

(3) Types of sharing on the system:

Do users need to share data files and programs, or do they need to share expensive peripherals such as laser printers or plotters? Are the peripherals the main issue, or do people really need to share applications programs (word processing, database-management programs, spreadsheets) and have almost immediate access to the same files? Sharing devices can almost always be accomplished with a cheaper switching system. Sharing programs or working on the same data file at the same time requires a more complex network environment.

(4) Local or mainframe connections:

Does the library staff need peer-to-peer communication (as in electronic mail), or is the primary need to connect to a host mainframe computer? Is the library connected to a large mainframe computer for accounting, personnel records, registrations, or online catalog services, or is library computing mainly stand-alone personal computers used for specific functions?

(5) Location of the network:

Where is the local area network going to be located? Is it needed in a single office area, on one floor of a facility, or in several campus buildings? Generally the more area covered, the more expense in terms of signal repeaters, special cable, or other transmission equipment.

(6) Cost reduction factors:

Is a major goal of networking the possible reduction in costs resulting from computing capability being provided at lower cost per user? For example, personal computers without disk drives can be connected to the network without loss of access to files or programs. In some situations, terminals can be connected to the main workstation file server without providing local computing capacity. Budget considerations also include the costs of network software and workstation operation and maintenance: "Anything you plug in will break or wear out."

(7) Increased flexibility:

Is the flexibility created by providing several processing and equipment options justified? If the staff has access to a greater array of applications programs and output devices, there may be an increase in creative use of personal-computer capacities in the library. There may also be an increase in time spent dreaming up things to do with the application programs.

(8) Overcoming maverick tendencies:

Is the library director seeking to reduce maverick tendencies in which everyone has his or her own way of doing word processing, database development, and telecommunications? Policies and procedures relating to equipment, software, and databases will be needed.

Conclusion

The library director will have to decide the goals of library involvement in local area networks with workstations. The library staff may be:

changing the ways in which they currently do business by reducing paper work, improving productivity of support staff, and enhancing the decision-making process

getting into a new business, utilizing workstations to provide new services to patrons

altering the social and economic structure of the library by providing to business and government value-added services for which a fee can be charged

Knowing *why* the library needs to get into local area networking and workstations is of critical importance. Once the goals and objectives of this involvement have been clarified, the planning process for implementing a local area network with workstations can begin. Chapter 2 focuses on this implementation process, especially on managing the human side of the operation, including issues in designing and supervising workstation areas.

Further Reading

Agosti, M. 1988. Is hypertext a new model of information retrieval? In *Proceedings of the 12th International Online Meeting, London, December 6-8, 1988*. Oxford: Learned Information, 57-62.

Broering, N. C. 1989. Enhancing library services with the Macintosh. In *Macintoshed libraries 2.0.*, ed. Bill Vaccaro and E. J. Valauskas. Cupertino, Calif.: The Apple Library Users Group, 1-4.

Chen, Ching-chih. 1989. *Hypersource on multimedia/hypermedia technologies*. Chicago: Library and Information Technology Association, American Library Association.

Ertel, M. 1989. Hypercard for libraries. *Apple Library Users Group Newsletter* 7 (January): 67-70.

———, and Oros, J. 1989. A tour of the stacks: Hypercard for libraries. *Online* 13 (January): 45-53.

Mackey, K. J. 1989. Automating overdues in a non-automated library: The Hypercard solution [at Converse College]. *College & Research Library Newsletter* 50(1): 23-27.

Shaw, S. J. 1988. Using microcomputers to train library staff. *Library Software Review* 7 (January-February):32.

Shill, H. B. 1987. Bibliographic instruction: Planning for the electronic information environment. *College & Research Libraries* 48 (May): 433-53.

2
Planning and Managing: The Human Factor

People are more expensive than technology. In the past, data processing hardware cost millions of dollars and required huge investments of money, space and facilities. Now, microcomputers are available at a fraction of the cost of one year of personnel time and are small enough to sit on an individual desk. Customized software can cost many times the price of the machine.

The new technology is increasingly user-friendly. Data processing specialists are less necessary than they were in the past for retrieving and analyzing information. More and more users will interface directly with their own data.

[Andriole, 1985, p. 252]

When an organization is faced with technological change, numerous technical details and equipment questions arise. Sometimes the people who will operate that equipment are forgotten. This chapter will consider the general impact of technological change on people, the workplace, and society. Next, the discussion turns to ways the library manager can work with people to plan and implement the use of workstations and local area networks in the library.

Change: The Essential Factor

From a management perspective, the central issue in the human-machine equation is the management of *change*. The new technologies are introducing new equipment, new processes and methods, new human relationships, and new work assignments and responsibilities. These changes mean that almost all aspects of the librarian's workplace may be changed. Many people view change as unusual or terrible rather than as a regular part of life. Indeed, a great deal of effort is put into making things stay the same. Some managers feel that as change happens the staff will divide into those who support change and those who oppose change.

The pace of technological change in current society is so rapid that many people feel technology is driving the workplace and that the equipment is taking precedence over the people. People tend to view technology as either: (1) bad—because it wastes resources, centralizes control, causes loss of personal freedom and dignity, and increases inequality, consumerism, de-skilled jobs, and eventual unemployment, or (2) good—because it causes increased personal freedom, more participation, more leisure time, more knowledge, and improved quality of life. There are certainly examples of both views found in libraries. The changes introduced by workstations and local area networks will effect the ways in which the library's business is done, what the library's *real* business will be in the future, the society in which the library operates, and finally, the pace of change. The effect of workstations and local area networks in each of these areas is discussed in the sections which follow.

How Librarians Do Business

Technology dramatically effects the way in which the library's business is transacted. Computers do jobs previously done by people (adding numbers, producing documents, creating graphics, and so on). Some individuals have developed skills in these areas that are now not only obsolete, but also more expensive than computer-produced products. Library staffers may wonder if their jobs are going to be lost because the computer now does part of the work. Other employees may feel that they cannot learn the new way to do work. Still other staff members may feel devalued by the introduction of technology. Some of the staff may fear that their previously valued skills (such as manual filing, typing, organizing information, public contact) are going to be useless and, at the very least, unappreciated. One way to insure these feelings is to announce in meetings that technology— especially workstations and local area networks—will cut the personnel costs of the library.

Not everyone in our society is excited about technological change. Some people fear that technology, in any form, devalues human life and that somehow people who must work with technological devices are "dehumanized" by the process. Many library staffers will remember B-grade movies about monster machines and robots (and computers) that go wrong. *2001* presented us with HAL (one letter earlier in the alphabet than IBM), which did go wrong in a violent and tragic way. Even the sequel, *2010,* did not overcome that image entirely. Individuals who have access to budget-planning or accounting figures, may compare the amount of capital outlay that any workstation-LAN system requires and decide that people will have to go if the budget is to be balanced. If individuals begin to make lists of those who will probably go, morale has already gone. Even if such ideas only enter the rumor stage, they have a negative impact on what the staff anticipates.

Figure 3 illustrates some potential responses to change as individuals evaluate the impact of a proposed change on themselves.

The evaluation of each individual is dependent on: (1) the amount of information he or she has about the change, (2) the extent to which he or she can participate in the decision-making process about the change, (3) how much the initiator of the change is trusted, and (4) the individual's past experience with change. Thus, the amount of resistance to changes brought on by workstations and local area networks is largely dependent on the climate of the organization.

Librarians who have worked with computers in the library will be the most likely to accept the new systems and processes necessary to make library workstations and local area networks operate successfully. In my experience with graduate students, older people have more anxiety about *any* kind of technology when it is introduced into the classroom or the library. If this original anxiety can be overcome, many people are willing to learn about these technologies and how to use them.

Even the most willing staff members who have very positive attitudes about computer-related technology may be frustrated by the necessity of sitting at a terminal for long periods of time, waiting for the computer, or having something unexpected happen while they are working. People are concerned about costs—what will this change cost me in time and dollars? People want to know what the impact of the technology system will be on

---

Figure 3.
Potential Responses to Change from an Individual Standpoint

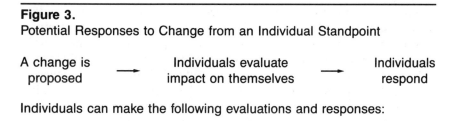

A change is proposed → Individuals evaluate impact on themselves → Individuals respond

Individuals can make the following evaluations and responses:

Evaluation	Response
Destructive	Resist opening
Threatening	Resist covertly
Uncertain	Tolerate
Positive	Support, participate

Andriole (1985, p. 290)

their work routines and their relationships with other workers (and their families). People may also worry that they do not have the ability to learn how to use the system effectively.

Library employees may feel that the changes have been introduced because library managers do not appreciate the staff's abilities or style. Some library staff members have had experience with computers, online services, and word processing, while other workers (because of assignment or personal preference) have not. Unless the whole staff can be oriented and trained to some basic level of understanding, those who have the knowledge and experience will get more, and the others will justifiably feel left out. This information-rich/information-poor dichotomy can work against well-planned training efforts. If the staff is trained without regard to past experience, those who have experience may intimidate those who have none. Even the informed discussion that takes place before a staff-development activity can have this intimidating effect when some staff members "share" their previous computer experiences.

Libraries have moved to use technology in their operations but have not always considered the consequences for employees. Dakshinamurti (1985, p. 343) notes: "Library organizations were in such a hurry to be included in this (technological) transformation that few contemplated the resulting effect of computer-aided systems on their employees."

Staff Inclusion in Planning

Since the introduction of local area networking technology will effect working processes at all levels of the library, it is important that all staff members be involved in the process of deciding on a LAN system, its uses, and its installation. The process of involving the library staff in the planning of workstations and local area networking will depend on the planning style of the library management. Some organizations depend on detailed plans with highly structured schedules and carefully defined staff assignments. Other styles depend more on an information "brainstorming" planning method. Training for all levels of staff about anticipated changes *before they occur* is essential—employees deal more effectively with known changes.

The staff should be involved in the discussion of what areas of work the technology will affect, the variety of technological resources that may be utilized, and the process by which the choice of technologies is made. Training for use of the new technology does not need to mean hiring external resource people exclusively. If the concept of "training the trainers" is used, outside resource people can train a core group of staff who can then train the rest of the staff on a more gradual basis.

The Positive Effects of Change

On the positive side, workstations and local area networks allow people to do work they could not do before: contact persons at remote sites, order by computer, simulate dangerous situations, and provide information in graphic or pictorial form. People need to spend less time on tedious report writing, accounting details, and hand-drawing of graphs and charts. More time can then be spent on understanding the information with which they work—where it comes from, what it means, where it is going. Possible positive and negative organizational effects of local area networks are shown in Table 2.

In organizations where input to decision making from all levels of the organization is desirable, such a trend will be beneficial. As the extent of

Table 2.
Positive and Negative Organizational Effects of Local Area Networks

Affected Area	Positive Effects	Negative Effects
Work quality	wide data access, fewer lost items, wider participation in creating and reviewing data	indeterminate or mediocre data quality, reduced independence and initiative
Productivity	more work handled by more powerful equipment	greater resources used for inconsequential work
Employee changes	improved skills, more challenge, reduced status distinctions	fewer jobs for marginal performers, less personal interaction not enough status distinction
Decision-making effectiveness	quicker access to relevant facts, greater analytic capability, more staff involved in hunch-building and testing	too many facts to process, "forest and tree" problem, can encourage "group think"
Organizational structure	more effective decentralization	decentralization can get out of control
Costs	overall cost reductions	overall cost increase with vague benefits used as justification
Total impact	planning of new approaches	creates increased complexity and poorly functioning dependence relationships

Stallings (1987, p. 6)

automation increases, hierarchial administrative structures tend to flatten because of increased ease of communication at all levels, and the flatter organization tends to have a greater rate of change. Support staff tend to be involved in activities that previously were limited to professional staff members. In organizations where sources of decision-making information are closely guarded and decisions are decreed, such a trend can be organization-threatening. Personal computers hooked together for sharing information are basically communication devices. Where improved communication is really wanted, they can be most useful.

Information that was once collected, organized, and reported by specialists is increasingly being manipulated and interpreted by the end users themselves. Work patterns and control of the decision-making process are changing. *Scientific American* (1989, p. w1) introduces a special section on "the workstation revolution" with these words:

> Every year new stories about the emergence of faster, more functional, and, in defiance of generations of economists, cheaper computers appear. And every year come new claims that we are in the midst of a revolution. We are in the midst of a revolution. It is not simply because computers are getting smaller and cheaper. The word revolution implies something more dramatic.

> The computer revolution is about the fundamental change occurring in the relationship between human beings and computers. The way we work with computers is changing dramatically. In this revolution, the workstation has become the most visible agent of change.

Managing the Human Factor

Since staff stress in the face of change is predictable, the library manager can anticipate a number of potential problems and deal with them before any network choice or installation. Several steps are essential and require some detailed explanation, which is presented in the six sections that follow.

(1) Demonstrate knowledge of and concern about the work of all the staff

The library director and his or her staff need to demonstrate that they know the jobs people do and care about the work the rest of the staff is doing. Often the question is, "Does the boss know and care about what I do?"

Brod (1984, p. 180) suggests several dimensions of present and future work design that need to be taken into account:

> knowledge—are workers' skills being fully used in their present jobs? Is their work sufficiently challenging? Do they want more opportunity to learn new things?

psychology—are workers receiving sufficient recognition? Are needs for achievement being met? Is there room for advancement?

efficiency—is the work exhausting? Is the degree of accuracy required excessive? Is sufficient information provided for maximum job effectiveness?

task structure—is there sufficient variety in the work? Are workers given enough scope to use their own initiative? Are they provided with a chance to make planning suggestions?

ethics—does management look after the interests of its employees? Do managers convey respect for the skills of the workers? How do workers perceive top management and its goals?

The larger the organization, the more important it is to take public notice of the work of *all* subordinates on the staff and the contribution that work makes to the overall goals and objectives of the library. Taking credit for a job well done should always involve giving most of the credit to others. That is the nature of management—managers not do work, they get others to work. As Hutchins (1947, p. 138) said long ago:

> The administrator should never do anything he does not have to do, because the things he will have to do are so numerous that he can not possibly have time to do them. . . . He should never do anything he can get anybody to do for him. He should have the largest number of good associates he can find.

The creation of "good associates" at all levels of the library is the basic task of library directing.

As the planning process for technological change proceeds, everyone should be able to identify what his or her role will be in the emerging structure. When everyone's role and responsibilities are clear, the staff can function more effectively. Part of the staff-development process should include a review of the library's history of change as a means of acknowledging how this staff (and their predecessors) survived and perhaps even thrived on change. The library manager needs to be frank about his or her motives in suggesting the change—what are the "rewards" or benefits this change will bring about and why are they important to the library? Sharing of the experience of other library organizations that have gone through similar technological changes can also be helpful. Even sharing of "horror stories" of other libraries can give the staff confidence, "Well! We certainly will be able to do better than that."

Major reassurances that should be stressed repeatedly are that learning the new systems will take some time and that work flow may be slowed during the process. All too often a technology is introduced to "improve work-flow performance," which it may do in the longer run, but cannot do until people know how to use it and are comfortable with it. Since libraries must remain open during specific hours, and continue to serve their clients, library managers have several options during the training period:

hire additional temporary staff to handle some functions while the staff is in training

identify staff members who are very proficient at using the system and temporarily reassign them as trainers

hire outside organizations to do training for staff members. This option may offer the incentives of academic credit (i.e., for community college or university classes) or ease of scheduling (after-work hours).

(2) Remember the psychological denial processes at work in any social setting

Faced with the possibility of problems, obstacles, and resistance, librarians—like all other people—develop their own denial systems. The tendency of people who have had positive experience with personal computers and related technology is to assume that such experience is the normal thing and that everyone will naturally want to become involved in learning about these new and wonderful tools. As such people have more experience with technology, they develop an array of "shortcuts" (both in operations and language) which make great sense to them and absolutely no sense to the uninitiated.

Denial also influences staff, who will deny to themselves and others how they really feel about changes in operations, new equipment, different report forms, etc. Some steps can be taken to deal with denial phenomenon: encourage discussion of the proposed changes, give illustrations in meetings of how people might feel, and, above all, allow time for free discussion.

(3) Find out how people really feel about their work situation and the present equipment and technology they are using

Often the people who use typewriters, files, and telephones have excellent insights as to the usefulness and limitations of these tools. Their ideas about improvements in the work flow and needed equipment capabilities can be helpful in determining what types of workstations and local area networks (if any) are needed. Allowing the staff to participate in planning of workstation and local area network systems and in assisting with the selection of applications programs and standards provides a way of enriching the work life of the staff. People can acquire information from other individuals working at their peer level in other institutions; they can acquire new and more complex skills; they can make good decisions about what application to use for what purpose; and finally, they can be rewarded.

(4) Avoid the tendency to act like systems are fun and easy to use and that people are the problem

Personal computer systems that work efficiently and allow an information process to develop effectively are exciting. After an individual has worked hard to make a system work and it does, there is a natural "high." Often these feelings are not shared by the onlookers. The first time a spreadsheet program actually demonstrates its usefulness in selecting an appropriate purchase, or identies cost centers which need further study— and then provides a graph of the results which can be incorporated into a report—the individual working with the system may view the system in a very warm and friendly way. When staff members are resistant, seem to refuse to learn new operations, or passively fail to take part in planning, the attraction of the efficient machine is very strong.

However, library managers do not have the freedom to become personal-computer or network mavericks doing their own computing. For a library workstation/local area network system to work, all of the people with personal computers on their desks must be using the system to communicate and to improve the work process. No library can afford to support two information work-process systems (the way we used to do it and the way we are supposed to do it now). The bulk of the manager's time will be spent helping, encouraging, and cajoling staff into moving more and more of their work operations into the workstation/local area network environment.

For example, when a secretary has both a workstation with attached printer and a typewriter, there is a tendency to still use the typewriter for envelopes, memos, and "short things." Yet applications software is available (and is mounted on my own personal computer) to allow envelope addressing, label making, and memo typing exactly like the typewriter. This software can be operated, even while I am working on the draft of this book, without changing the word-processing program or the printer in any way. A number of secretaries in the university have been introduced to this software and encouraged to use it—to the point that at least two have almost stopped using the typewriter altogether. Assisting staff in developing the skills and providing the appropriate applications software for their use is the one major job of the manager.

Even managers are not free from the problem. Applications software now exists to allow the secretary to maintain calendars for all the staff and create daily or weekly calendar sheets that fit into the now-popular *Action Planner* notebooks. In several years of consultation work, I have yet to find a library-management group or a public-school administrative group that took eagerly to the idea of maintaining a calendar in this way. People forgot to tell the secretary about appointments, refused to allow the secretary to schedule appointments, or ignored the printed daily calendars. If a common calendar system is used by professional staff on a local area network, scheduling becomes much simpler, and conflicts in meeting times are eliminated. The library manager can model appropriate behavior by instructing the secretary to keep his or her calendar, by referring to that calendar when making an appointment, and encouraging others to refer to his or her calendar on the network when they want to schedule events. Otherwise, the manager can continue to keep a desk calendar and not use the system.

(5) View the development and use of workstations and local area networks as a long-term planning and evaluation project, involving people as the opportunity arises

Since not everyone will enthusiastically support change, the manager can use the planning period that precedes installation of a workstation/local area network system to identify those work groups in the library who are either most interested or most in need of the services such a system can provide. Few organizations will be able to bring their system up "all at once." If the library director and staff do a careful analysis of work groups and needs, they will be able to identify areas where current information flow is slowed (or even blocked), as well as areas where the departmental or work group is eager to get involved. Starting with areas of critical need or eagerness, the library director can involve several units in detailed planning, pilot operations, training seminars, etc.

When departments or work groups do a good job making use of the workstations and the local area network, the library manager needs to be sure that everyone (staff, board of trustees, etc.) knows about how well they are doing. This "island culture" idea has been successfully used in many institutions and is celebrated in Peters and Austin's *A Passion for Excellence* (1985). If the people using the system seem to be able to make it work for them in their jobs and seem to be enjoying it, other staff groups may want to get into the act. Many agencies use an "electronic newsletter" on the local area network to announce new applications, to praise effective users, and to share solutions to problems bothering everyone on the system.

The library manager will also need to be aware of what Hannigan (1988, p. 216) calls the "curve of nonsatisfaction," as workstation and local area networks continue to be used. This move toward dissatisfaction with the system(s) is usually made up of:

increased breakdown of hardware
increased software failures
increased data loss
voiced dissatisfaction with software

reported system slowdowns
requests for additional and more complex data manipulation and reporting
suggestions for purchase of peripherals
increased requests for machine replacement
requests for newer or enhanced version of software
reports of frustration because the system does not meet user needs
breakthrough technology making current architecture obsolete

Since this curve of dissatisfaction seems inevitable, the library manager needs to evaluate system operations from the users' perspective and try to anticipate staff concerns and budget requirements for replacement, enhancement, and conversion to newer systems. Information on how the system is working and what particular problems are occurring can provide feedback to long-range planning for solutions before problems get out of hand.

A part of this long-range planning process is the development and announcement of a consistent, humane policy on how the technology of workstations and local area networks is going to be used. This policy needs to clearly state that the library (or other institution) recognizes the psychological needs of the staff and takes those factors into account in designing and assigning work. Jobs are to match people, not people jobs.

People vary in their ability to process information with any technology (pencil, typewriter, telephone, computer). The employee and his or her immediate supervisor are the best judges of the capabilities in this area. Not everyone will produce the same amount of data (or completed telephone calls). People also vary in their ability to "stick" with a task. Some individuals are not able to monitor their own work pace and need assistance in knowing when to stop and take a break. Some individuals will work at high speed in short bursts, others will be slower but will continue a consistent rate of production over a longer period of time. Institutional policy should allow for such variances.

The basic principle of policy should be a balance between productivity and worker well-being. The latter can be enhanced if the job design allows for some type of challenge to be built into workstation and local area network tasks. Work that is too simple breeds boredom and may even cause hostility. Where workers have the opportunity to learn new skills and assume new responsibilities, they have a sense of contributing to the organization as a whole.

In the workstation/local area network environment, such new opportunities include: (1) the ability to do more complex editing, even with less-than-excellent spelling skills, thanks to spell-checking software, (2) the ability to produce pleasing graphics, charts, and designs with desktop publishing software, (3) the ability to handle mathematical and accounting information without a calculator or pencil by using spreadsheet software, (4) the ability to take on systems-level responsibility when assigned the task of backing up files on a regular basis, and (5) the ability to "test" the system, using appropriate software, and discover what needs to be fixed. Naturally, managers can do all of these tasks, but if they delegate them and recognize work well done, the worker's job has become more valuable to the whole institution.

(6) Realize that the major focus of a library can be changed by the workstation/local area network system

Any time work is done on computers, there is the possibility of monitoring work flow. One of the latest developments in this area is the monitoring of office telephone use, which allows a manager to know what numbers are called and how long the calls last. Almost any processing function can be measured in some units.

For work (or nonwork) to be done without being seen or evaluated becomes increasingly difficult in a workstation environment. Anything sent through electronic circuits can be measured in some way. Library managers need to consider the morale impact of these possibilities as well as the work-flow analysis possibilities. This monitoring capacity can produce a great deal of stress in the workplace. In the computerized workplace, people may develop stress symptoms because they feel that the control of their jobs (and lives) is distant, centralized, and mechanical. Brod (1984, p. 44) illustrates this trend:

> At some American Express offices, a computer monitors the time taken by employees to answer the telephone. If there are more than three rings the computer notifies the supervisor. VDT operators at Blue Cross/Blue Shield in San Francisco have their keystrokes tallied automatically. Each time they go to the bathroom, their count stops and their keystroke-per-hour rate dips. The mere fact that this kind of surveillance is being conducted promotes uneasiness and strain.

Often managers see local area networks as a means of cost reduction and higher quality of work. Properly trained and motivated staff members want to, and will, provide improved work. Ideally, supervisors observing employees' work bring to their jobs some understanding and empathy for the individuals they oversee. Being supervised by a person with whom you can communicate is different from being supervised by a software program set to a specific production standard.

While such monitoring of work flow (or patron requests) can lead to more efficient (and hopefully effective) work, it is also possible for staff members to react to "being watched all the time." Skillful communication about the reasons for the monitoring and involvement of staff members in the discussions and decision making related to the monitoring are essential.

Responsibility for Business in the Future

Radical technological changes may mean that librarians can attempt to do jobs they never contemplated before. Portable computers allow branch and extension librarians to make reports and requests away from the main library, speed up deliveries, and improve information flow while reducing paperwork. Managers can have regular contact through electronic mail or teleconferencing, thus reducing face-to-face meetings (and costs). If the library's use of computers changes the kinds of information the library acquires, or the user population, some of the staff may be uncomfortable with new formats of information and with meeting the requests of the new user groups.

The changing technology will affect the supervision of work in libraries. Customer preferences can quickly be identified. Product scanning at the check-out line in supermarkets has provided an extremely fine-tuned inventory-control system. Products can be quickly evaluated in terms of their turnover in sales. Those products which do not turn over rapidly enough are eliminated from the next order. This inventory-control technique explains why some items such as various types of pasta and breakfast cereal have disappeared from the grocer's shelves. Relatively inexpensive circulation programs like *CIRCULATION PLUS* by Follett can provide excellent circulation-data reports and inventory control for acquisitions, weeding, and general collection management in any library collection up to sixty-five thousand volumes (larger collections possible in 1989). Inventory control systems allow for the monitoring of specific library activities (including main library and branches). Potential problems can be easily pinpointed. Peters (1988, p. 637) issues the following warning:

> Implementation of the new integrated information technology-based systems is much more difficult than anyone dreamed. For one thing, it turns out that the installation of such systems is not primarily a matter of technology. It is a matter of organization. *Every power relationship, inside and outside the firm, is affected by the installation of the new information technology systems.*
> [author's emphasis]

Hannigan (1988, pp. 207–208) points out that selection of the individual to plan microcomputer and local area network operations in the library environment can directly impact the staff view of the whole process:

> The selection and appointment of a particular staff member . . . may convey a subtle message to staff that is neither anticipated or desired. For instance, if the person is a very junior staff member, the appointment may be perceived as demonstrating a casual attitude on the part of higher administration. If the person is a so-called techie, the project may assume a mystique that is unnecessary. . . . And

if the director of the project is highly placed in the administration, the other staff members may be either inspired, or fear displacement. Thus, a key factor to success at this juncture is adequate communication.

Even in the simplest library, someone must be responsible for planning policies for the system and procedures for the operation of that system. If data are going to be transferred between two computers, those computers must not be used for some other purpose (or turned off) while transfer is taking place. In situations where a telephone system is part of the transfer process, those telephones must be "safe" from interruption, or disconnection by third parties. Mechanical printer-selection systems cannot be switched or turned off while someone else is using the printer.

As more complex local area networks involving five to ten microcomputers are contemplated, keeping network rules becomes critical. Policies must all be implemented on handling data files, getting the system restarted when it "crashes," deciding when routine maintenance is to be done, and specifying what data is available to what operators (security). Typically, someone must be placed in charge of the network. That someone will be responsible for:

establishing and monitoring policies
trouble-shooting when there are problems
training new users of the system and retraining others
arranging for maintenance and upgrading as needed
insuring that regular backup of data files are made
insuring that old files are removed regularly
monitoring needs for new equipment, capabilities, and software

The responsibilities of the network administrator can be detailed in the various phases of designing, implementing, and operating the network, as illustrated in Figure 4.

Planning for Workstations and LANs

Does the library really need a local area network? The library director and staff need to avoid "me-too-ism" in implementing workstation/local area network systems. Just because another library system is networked, does not justify a local area network for any given library. Finding answers to the following questions during the planning process will help the library staff make appropriate decisions.

(1) What kind of files need to be exchanged?

Files may be word processing (text), spreadsheets (numerical), special-format files such as desktop-publishing or graphics files, or there may be

Figure 4.
Details of Network Administrator's Responsibilities

Design Phase

prepare lists of hardware and software resources (what we have,
 what we need)
identify current and potential users and specify output devices
 needed
physically lay out the network, including interconnections (gateways)
 to other networks
develop needed names conventions for network and device names
order network hardware and applications programs and secure
 licensing agreements where needed

Implementation Phase

install and test network hardware (supervise if contracted)
load network software on each microcomputer node
load applications software and test
make backup copies of necessary files
test network software from each node
train users in network use, electronic mail, applications, and output
 devices (printers)

Operations Phase

periodically back up central files (or assign this task)
restore user configurations, data, applications files
upgrade software as needed
inform users of new network features and device resources
notifiy users of network problems, equipment failure
review needed moves and changes in network, nodes, and
 interconnections
update network hardware as needed
expand network when capabilities are available and expansion is
 needed

(Kleeman, et al., 1986, adapted from p. 151)

files now exchanged in paper format that do not need to be exchanged at all. Many libraries carefully weed their materials collection before bar coding and data entry in circulation and online catalog systems; the staff can use the same process to evaluate the current file-exchange program. Why does this person need this file of information? If people do not use the files they now receive, why place those files in a local area network system?

(2) How often does file exchange take place?

Not all files in a library have the same time value. Some information needs to get to everyone at once. Other information may not need to be exchanged more than quarterly or annually. Probably a lot of information files do not need to be exchanged at all. Simply measuring the volume of paper information files does not tell the staff how often that information needs modification and exchange.

(3) How many different systems do we now have, and can they be connected or integrated?

The library staff needs to inventory the current methods of creating information files, exchanging them, and storing them. Such an inventory should include all of the paper as well as microcomputer and main-frame computer information-file systems. For example some libraries are connected to larger institutional computer systems for accounting, inventory control, and reporting. Or to cite another example, one area school-library operation is connected to an electronic mail system, a county government accounting system, and a remote-site bibliographic utility; and it maintains certain files on unconnected microcomputer systems. The more different systems and formats, the more problems will arise in creating a local area network system that can handle the various files and their formats satisfactorily.

(4) Do several people need access to the files simultaneously?

If librarians attend exhibits or workshops on local area networks, they will see demonstrations of simultaneous interaction in word processing, databases, spreadsheets, and graphics. They will even see systems where individuals can talk with one another and see one another (because of built-in TV equipment) as a part of the network. It is certainly fascinating to watch someone else modify the screen on which you are working. It may also have other less fortunate effects. People vary in work style. They may need to show a draft to someone else before publication. They may need to write text or numbers down, review them, modify them, and then share them. Simultaneous interaction with an application program demands high-speed transmission of data in the local area network and sophisticated software. The library staff needs to be sure that the expense of faster, more sophisticated systems is justified by the work being done in the library. Often a sequence of "I do a draft, you look at it and make comments, I redraft, and we ask for comments" will work just as well on a simpler system.

(5) Will creating a local area network mean that people have to learn new applications programs or disk-operating systems?

If the library staff (at any level) is already using applications programs and microcomputers, the staff planning a new local area network needs to compare the screen-display commands of the various network systems and those now used by staff. If these system commands are similar, it will be easier for staff to learn the new system, and the director will encounter less resistance to it. If possible, application programs now in use should be put on the network. Only as a last resort, and because a network version of the software is not available, should the library staff be asked to learn a new network system and new word-processing and database programs.

(6) What kind of security system must be installed to limit access?

Sensitive data in the library system will include information about people working in the library, some budget and accounting information, and patron records. When such data is placed on a network, the network administrator will need to invoke password systems at two levels: (a) who has access to *read* this information? and (b) who has access to *modify* this information?

Part of developing a security system for the network will be the determination of what files need security. Obviously not all of the files in the system will need to be protected from general access. In fact, many files are created so everyone on the staff can have access to them: announcements, job vacancies, general news, congratulations, etc. While the library manager is thinking about general-access files, he or she should also be thinking about how such files get updated and deleted. A general-access file subsystem can be like a vertical file in the library: everyone puts things in, but no one is responsible for cleaning out the files.

Once general-access files have been determined, the process of defining security levels begins. Some files contain sensitive or confidential information about staff or patrons (including patron circulation records and individual salary information). These files must be accessible only to those who need the information to do their jobs. Other files are management planning and budget files and may need to be secured.

Many network systems provide password security for specific files and applications programs. Even some of the operating-system menu programs provide password security for specific applications. Such simple security systems are often used to prevent accidental erasing of disks (including hard disks), or modification of data in files that are used for archival or benchmark information. Many systems now provide several levels of security including both a password and a system-user ID number.

(7) Who will be involved in the planning and design process for the local area network?

The library director and his or her staff must engage in a planning effort as workstations and LANs are considered. That planning effort will attempt to answer the questions raised above and will be directed toward: keeping costs under control and dealing with inevitable growth in the system.

Involving the library staff in the process (as suggested earlier in this chapter) is *not* the same as letting everyone decide what equipment and software they want. Very different needs can be met through the purchase of consistent hardware and software. Indeed, the work people need to do has become increasingly independent of specific brands of personal computers and networks. Most of the necessary applications programs and graphics can now be had in several different equipment brands. Librarians should not make the mistake of thinking that use of a laser printer or desktop publishing software requires a particular brand of workstation. Information gathered from the staff about what work is now done by whom will help the director determine what kinds of equipment and software are necessary.

The library director can assume that the system's use will be greater than he or she expects. The only local area networks that do not create increasing demand are those that do not work very well or are hard to use. For several decades a rule in academic computing was that low demand for services means a system that is hard to use and not well managed. A successful local area network (or computer system) always exceeds its capacity to respond in an amazingly short span of time. If the system is compatible with current applications software the staff is using, if the menu screens displayed by the system are understandable, and if a command issued to the system brings about the anticipated response, staff members will quickly find new ways to place demands on the system.

The individual in charge of network acquisition and maintenance can anticipate several growth problems by:

buying extra workstations and controller cards

making sure that the system can support more workstations (double whatever the plans say)

purchasing a file server big enough to have lots of slots, a fast-operating system, and a capacity to add disk space, tape backup (automatic)

being sure that the creation of "temporary" or "guest" log-ons is easy so that anyone can be assigned a station on a temporary basis while their station is being fixed.

(8) Who is responsible for documenting every decision in planning, purchasing, and installation of the system?

Once the planning team has made a decision, it should be recorded, together with its justification. A record should be kept of whatever is bought or leased. All documentation and correspondence, agreements, and technical-support information should be saved in an organized file. The manager of the network should have an up-to-date floor plan showing workstations, cable routes, and access points.

A log of problems during installation, testing, and operation should be kept, as well as a record of what steps the manufacturer, vendor, or local maintenance provider took to deal with the problems. If the network system is using the telephone lines of an organization, a layout of the telephone system is critical. Telephone layouts are changed on a regular basis. Rarely are old, unused lines removed. Connecting a network to a telephone line that goes nowhere is not helpful.

(9) What training needs develop as the uses of the workstations and local area network become clear?

When a library buys a network system, the staff should check out training possibilities with both company and independent groups. Training for use of a local area network and its associated workstations is not a one-time event. Since personal computers and local area networks will be operated by people, the library director and his or her staff cannot ignore the impact of new systems on the work flow in the library and the people involved in that work flow. People have made the manual library system work (or not work very well), and people will be needed to make the network system work.

Many computer applications arose during that time when most microcomputing was done by only a few individuals in an organization—individuals who often used their own microcomputers and shared their applications software with other mavericks. As a result, where the professional staff members have their own machines, and no policies on applications software have been developed, it is likely there are three or four different word-processing systems, several types of desktop and disk-utility programs, and several individually acquired software packages in use. Such individualism is all right so long as the products shared are in print-copy form. When the need to share information earlier than the print-copy stage becomes important (as in spreadsheets, databases, and drafts of policy statements) then the library staff needs the same applications software.

People who have been doing "maverick" personal computing will have developed styles of work and intense likes and dislikes related to personal computers, printer types, and applications programs. Someone has said that users of the Macintosh regard it as a religious artifact, not a work-processing station.

(10) Who will be responsible when I'm gone?

Who can do the job if the assigned person is gone? Since networking (and microcomputing) often begins without planning and just grows without evaluation, it is possible to create a situation in which the critical person on a staff does not have a backup. Sometimes the critical person is someone who knows how to do the job, but cannot teach others how to do it. Sometimes the critical person does not know what procedures really work, but tries a variety of possible solutions until one does. Often these people carry a great deal of vital information in their heads and tool boxes.

(11) How is the information on the network protected?

In the stand-alone environment of microcomputing, the loss of a file means a headache for one individual who must reconstruct the file or who fortunately may have a backup file with most of the data intact. Everyone who has done any computing knows the value of the motto "save files frequently, make backup disks often." Even so, individuals still lose files, delete the wrong files, damage disks, and encounter similar mishaps.

In the network environment, there are no *individual* files. Although some files may be secured from general access, everyone uses the network to create files, share files, and delete files. What is everyone's job is no one's job! Someone needs to be in charge of regular backup of network files. In most situations "regular" means daily. While individuals using microcomputers may retrieve and save an individual file on a removable disk, they do not usually go through the process of backing up all the files on the network file server. If the file-server function is shared among microcomputers so there is no overall file server, backing up of files can be even more complicated.

When people first start using hard disks on microcomputers or networks, they often assume that since the disk is not taken out of the system, it will run forever. This assumption is not true. Not only do hard disks fail (usually due to bearings wearing out), but the "low level" formatting of the disk can degrade to the point where access to files is impossible. If the file allocation table (FAT) is damaged, access to files is very difficult and requires the use of some type of file-recovery utility program. Since hard-disk drives can fail, the only reasonable alternative is to save vital information in another place: on a set of removable disks, or on a tape backup system.

Having someone assigned the responsibility to back up the system on a regular basis insures that valuable data, and sometimes applications programs, will not be lost. Often one copy of backup disks (or tape) is not enough. A duplicate set of data is often stored in a remote site so that damage by fire or water will not destroy "our only backup copy." Because backup is so important some vendors are now offering automatic backup systems, which create backup files on tape or at least warn the user of the system when a certain file (or set of files) has not been backed up recently.

As the capacity of removable disks has increased, the difficulties in making backups has decreased. For example, utilizing one of the backup programs and 1.45MK disks (3½-inch) means that 2 million bytes of information can be backed up on one disk.

If there are any nagging doubts about these questions during the planning process, the library planning team needs to get more information. It may be that a simple mechanical switch will overcome the backup of peripherals. People may not need to share data because their decision-making tasks involve very different data, or data that requires on-site modification or summarization.

There seems to be a myth in such business and service agencies as libraries that someone in the management system has data that (if shared) would solve a specific problem. Often the myth is based on the assumption that someone has that data or access to such data, when in fact the data in the needed format may not exist at all. Creating a local area network to access data that does not exist or that must be recomputed to be of any use is an expense that no library can afford. An equally dangerous myth is that computing or networking will cure bad data. There has been no change in the ancient rule: "garbage in, garbage out." Workstations attached to a local area network can only increase the rate of garbage pile-up if that is all that is available. Verifying information is still a human-management task.

Information essential to decision making in any institution flows through informal communication channels of the institution. Peters and Waterman's "managing by wandering around" (1982) takes the informal face-to-face communication processes very seriously. No arrangement of workstations and connections between them will create an automatic inclusion of informal information. If staff members are willing participants in planning and implementing the system, and if everyone has opportunities to take part in orientation visits, training activities, and evaluation of possible systems, then the electronic-mail system of the local area network may become the recognized channel for information and communication. Thus the library manager will have instant access to staff concern, suggestions, and problems identified by the early-warning system operated by staff members in every part of the library. The major resources for making any local area network operate successfully are the people working at the workstations in various parts of the library.

The Emerging Information Society

Computer and communications technology alters the society in which a library operates. More and more information about business and services is available through computers. Businesses, consumers, researchers, and citizens expect current information to be as close as their telephone. DeBuse (1988) identifies six key technological developments accelerating change:

(1) powerful and portable computers available in home, car, and office
(2) user-interface software with graphic interfaces and simple pointing devices (like the mouse) shared by most (if not all) of the computer industry
(3) optical storage storing up to 550 megabytes of data
(4) hypermedia (or hypertext) to organize and provide access to very large databases by creating and representing multiple levels and relations among parts (or concepts) of a database
(5) artificial intelligence to perform complex functions using expert systems to assist people in finding what they want
(6) authoring systems that permit the publication and use of hypermedia materials and other interactive publications or programs

He sees these six technologies creating a monumental shift in the ways knowledge is stored and communicated. As current word processing, imaging software, and communications systems have made the distribution of printed materials easier and faster, these technologies will assist in developing new ways to share data, create knowledge, and change it dynamically.

Where once people had to go by the bank and talk with someone, or later use the 24-hour teller machine, they can now call from any location using an 800-number and get the same information. Naturally such systems have security risks: what if someone has access to a social security number and four-digit bank card number? Then they have access to account information and also to the account at any 24-hour teller machine.

Some things can be communicated face-to-face that cannot be communicated through the computer. Social structures are affected by these differences. There is less filtering of information within the social structure of the organization. Top managers can now have access to salespersons and customers without the filtering effect of traditional management-information systems. Negative information (customers' complaints, actual sales records, delays in delivery, cost overruns) can no longer be hidden or delayed. Wright's law which states, "negative information does not flow uphill, because that's where the money comes from" can be overcome if the computer network allows managers to have access to information typically routed "through the system."

On the other end of the system, the worker with a computer can have access to sales figures, projections, and working documents (unless they are "secured" in the system). Data and interpretation of "how things are going" is much more widely spread throughout the system. Such open systems are effective in horizontal organizations, which require information and input from a variety of sources; these systems are not so widely accepted in more traditional hierarchical organizations.

Conclusion

Technology accelerates the rate of change within a business and in society. Workstations and local area networks will create demand for more and better technological innovations. Sometimes rapid technological change can have a freezing effect on human decision making.

Library managers who observe other institutions using a technology may notice only that the technology rapidly becomes obsolete and requires upgrading or replacement. Such managers may decide to wait until the pace of change slows down. They will have a long wait!

Every institution of society is changing more rapidly than was ever anticipated. The management skills of the future are related more to dealing with change and its required technologies than running the current institution well. Libraries are caught up in this change as technology gets introduced into all aspects of the library's operations. Steffen (1987, p. 126) points out: "Whether we are able to live with and manage change effectively will make the difference between the bright, vital future for libraries forecast by some and the bleak outlook predicted by others." The basic task of the library manager is to assist the entire staff in viewing change as a chance to learn, develop new skills, share with colleagues, and make positive changes in the library organization.

Further Reading

Anderson, D. J. 1986. Preparing people for change. In *Training issues in changing technology*. Chicago: Library Administration and Management Association, American Library Association, 15–22.

Berger, P. 1980. Managing revolutions: Coping with evolving information technologies. *Special Libraries* 71 (September): 386–97.

De Klerk, A., and Euster, J. R. 1989. Technology and organizational metamorphoses. *Library Trends* 37(4): 457–68.

Fine, S. 1986. Technological innovation, diffusion and resistance: An historical perspective. *Journal of Library Automation* 7 (Spring): 83–108.

Jones, D. E. 1989. Library support staff and technology: Perceptions and opinions. *Library Trends* 37(4): 432–56.

Lequire, W. 1983. Attitudes toward automation/innovation in academic libraries. *Journal of Library Automation* 8 (January): 344–51.

Marchant, M. P., and England, M. M. 1989. Changing management techniques as libraries automate. *Library Trends* 37(4): 468–83.

Olsgaard, J. N. 1985. Automation as a socio-organizational agent of change: An evaluative literature review. *Information Technology and Libraries* 4 (March): 19–28.

——. 1989. The physiological and managerial impact of automation on libraries, *Library Trends* 37(4): 484–94.

Person, R. J. 1986. Human factors in adopting library technology: An overview with an emphasis on training. In *Training issues in changing technology*. Chicago: Library Administration and Management Association, American Library Association, 1–14.

Presley, R., and Robinson, C. L. 1986. Changing roles of support staff in an online environment. *Technical Services Quarterly* 4 (Fall): 25–39.

Schroeder, J. K. 1986. Training today's library staff for tomorrow. In *Training issues in changing technology*. Chicago: Library Administration and Management Association, American Library Association, 45–52.

Sievert, M. E., et al., 1988. Investigating computer anxiety in an academic library. *Information Technology and Libraries* 7 (September): 243–52.

3

Workstation Applications

*If libraries are to survive as viable services, they must not only
understand the current computing and telecommunications technologies, but they must develop and execute plans to implement these
technologies. This is an issue at all levels: local, state, regional, and
national. Doing so will require money, talent, education, creativity,
determination, consensus, management, and most of all, vision.*
[Lynch and Brownrigg, 1986, p. 46]

Libraries use workstations for a wide variety of online and offline
services. Vendors have begun to offer personal computers or workstations as
a part of their package for various library functions: online catalogs, circulation, CD-ROM bibliographic retrieval, acquisitions. This chapter discusses workstations and local area networks in terms of the needs of library
managers and specific management functions that these systems serve.

General Considerations

Before reviewing specific library management needs and applications,
there are several general management factors which need examination:
(1) cost-benefit factors, and (2) workstation-use factors.

Cost-Benefit Factors

The major reason for considering workstations and local area networks
in library management is increased information management and communications efficiency. Workstations allow the library manager to find,
process, and disseminate information much more efficiently. When the
manager's workstation is tied to other workstations through a local area
network, that information managment and communications process becomes even more efficient. Text and numeric data, which once had to be
assembled by hand, can now be accessed using integrated word processing
programs. Analysis of operating efficiency in the library can be done at the

workstation using spreadsheet programs. Many repetitive tasks can be handled with minimum effort. Information from remote sites can be acquired easily through online database services. Higher-quality printed and graphics materials can be produced. Library managers can not only do what they did before; they can also do things that were not possible when everything was done by hand.

As the library-management staff begins to consider the introduction of personal computers or workstations into the library operation, or the integration of currently used equipment into a local area network, a basic library-management question is: can managers get easy access to the information that the various units of the library are generating at their workstations? There is no rationale for having information created in different formats by different programs so that the managers must handle the information as printed documents.

For example, when statistics are gathered and manipulated by spreadsheet programs, these statistics should be created by *one type* of spreadsheet program so that further management analysis and synthesis is possible without rekeying the data into a different system. Another example occurs when a library considers purchasing an online catalog or integrated library system. The system should allow for routine gathering of statistical summaries that can easily be utilized by managers for planning and evaluation of library operations. The format of these reports should be "importable" into whatever spreadsheet application programs the library is using. If a change in spreadsheet programs is required, the costs of new application programs and the staff training costs should be included in the overall cost estimates for the online catalog system. Some systems have the capability of running analysis programs on a regular basis and saving that analysis in a form that can be manipulated by available spreadsheet programs.

Such analysis is not limited to numerical data. Many organizations have maintained a correspondence file of copies (usually carbons) of all letters the organization staff has sent, to be reviewed by the management team on a regular basis. In the local area network environment, it is possible to create a correspondence archive file for the same purposes. Naturally, such a file serves no purpose if it is never read or weeded—indeed the file can become gigantic in a relatively short time. However, a careful analysis of such a file can uncover: (1) recurring questions in reference, (2) recurring problems or misunderstanding about library operations or policies, (3) library image problems created by correspondence, (4) problems with vendors, and (5) possible areas where form letters or responses can be created.

As the library moves into a local area network, any workstation on the system that is generating statistical data should be configured so that such data is available to the library management. On the other hand, some data collected should not be available to all workstations. In the local area network communications environment, the library-management staff will need to decide what types of information will routinely be collected and placed in management files for further study.

Marmion (1988) suggests another reason for considering workstations for various library-management applications: the workstation can be utilized for a variety of other functions when it is not busy with the the "purchased-for" application. For example, the IBM PC with hard disk purchased for use as the processor for a circulation system in a school media center can also be used for media-center management functions such as publicity materials, correspondence, budget analysis, collection management, and other data-base applications. If the hard-disk capacity is large enough, all these applications can be stored on the hard disk. In the *Wilsonline* workstation (PS/2 or older PC XT), the CD-ROM database can be used, *Wilsonline* can be called online, and various other online bibliographic databases can be contacted using the same machine.

In my library education department, the *Wilsonline* machine is also used for communication with the campus mainframe (via dial-up modem) for word processing of student papers and will eventually be attached to the campuswide broadband so that the university library online catalog will be accessible to faculty and students through that same workstation.

Sometimes these shared uses do conflict. Different uses may demand different configurations of software instructions. Memory-resident programs may also conflict for areas of RAM in the workstation, and various installed cards may need to have dip-switch adjustments to modify their starting addresses in the system. In some CD-ROM systems, each different vendor requires different configurations for the computer system—most having to do with how the CD-ROM device is to be treated as a disk drive and accessed. Sometimes the workstation will need to be restarted for each different database. In local area network situations, careful design of a common way to access different CD-ROM systems will be needed.

Workstation Use Factors

Library workstations that cost around three thousand dollars can be developed. Alternatively, such workstations can cost more than ten times that amount. Much of the cost will depend on the uses of the workstation. The library manager will need to develop some type of priority list of uses which will maximize the use of the workstation's capabilities without pushing the costs through the roof.

It is often true the the applications programs a secretary needs are more complex and powerful than those of a manager. Typically, the manager needs a quick and easy integrated program package that allows memo drafts, electronic mail, spreadsheet creation and analysis, and a calendar. Such integrated programs and "desk organizers" are available at low cost.

On the other hand, the secretary or assistant may need to convert the memo draft into a formal letter, add various standard paragraphs, retrieve parts of a spreadsheet for inclusion, and incorporate the library's logo in the final form of the letter or publication. He or she may even need to do a presentation graphic to go along with the other materials. As easy desktop publishing becomes available, the secretary may need a laser printer, page and font formatting applications programs, and hand or page-size scanning equipment that allows the digitizing of images for use with a variety of text-processing and desktop publishing programs. Many of the newer network-ready applications programs are not character-oriented like the traditional word-processing programs, but are graphics-oriented programs that allow the person designing the final product to view (in a variety of sizes) how the finished product will look. The library manager should properly be concerned about the content of produced materials and may wish to approve the design of the final product. However, the manager may not have time to design graphics or to load data into a complex spreadsheet and produce the graphs to be used to interpret that spreadsheet information. The general rule applies: transfer as many functions to other staff members as possible once basic management decisions have been made.

The library manager's workstation is his or her primary means of accessing information and applying it to various management projects. In designing a workstation for library management, the primary question is, "what information does the manager now need and what does he or she want to be able to do with that information?" It is likely that efficient, effective communication with the staff and the public and acquisition and manipulation of information for planning and evaluation are among the library manager's highest priorities.

If the library manager is going to use the workstation a great deal, it will need to have an excellent display monitor. Since much of the information gathered and reformatted for communication is saved, a large hard-disk storage capacity will be essential. There is nothing more frustrating than the message on the screen, "unable to save" due to lack of disk space. Because library managers need to do lots of different things at the same time, their workstations will need fairly high operating speed (80286 or 80386 chips), high-quality communications hardware and software, and the ability to communicate with a variety of printing devices. If the workstation is to be a stand-alone system, all of these items will need to be part of that workstation: large hard disk, high-speed modem, excellent monitor, and printer(s). When the workstation is part of a larger local area network, some of these items can be attached to the file server that serves all users of the network. Indeed, the major saving of a local area network is that expensive input and output devices and mass storage can be shared efficiently by a number of users.

The library manager will probably want to have the security of individual-station hard-disk storage and some kind of printer. The ability to create private files and see printout is essential. However, high-quality (laser) printing, graphics files and scanners, massive text and numerical files, and bibliographic data can be located at the remote file server. As the amount of information stored and communicated grows, the need for a centralized local area network will increase.

To sum up, the library manager's workstation should have excellent communication capability both in the library's local area network and with remote databases. That workstation should have hard-disk capability (forty megabytes or more), relatively high speed of operations, and some printing capability. Ease of use for managing should be a primary consideration.

Specific Applications

The library management will use workstations and local area networks for word-processing applications, planning, evaluation and budgeting applications, and communication and public relations applications. Each of these application areas is discussed below.

Word Processing

Library management communicates with a wide variety of publics through printed communication—letters, memorandums, public relations releases, and the like. Much of this correspondence is repetitive as the library responds in the same way to similar situations. Word-processing applications programs are ideally suited for such situations. If the library management staff keeps a chronological correspondence file, that file can be studied profitably to determine: (1) what types of correspondence this library routinely creates and (2) what correspondence formats are typically used.

Once these questions are answered, the management staff is ready to create content and "forms" for routine communication. Library managers reading this book should pause and reread the last two sentences. If the library manager does not know what parts of the library's communication are repetitive, the "create, store, and use again" advantages of word-processing packages will be lost. Libraries *do* tend to do things over and over again . . . even if each time the job is done as a new one. There are sources of routine communications and forms on disks that can be used. Many word-processing-applications publishers offer these disks. However, care should be taken with these preplanned communications and forms. Often the content and/or form are not appropriate for particular library operations or management styles.

Some librarians may object to form-type responses; however, a library that does not deal efficiently with routine communication will not be able to deal effectively or creatively with nonroutine communication. Creating routine responses and forms allows the delegation of such responses to support staff and gives professional management staff time to deal with other communications. Word-processing-applications programs allow for at least three types of routine communication: (1) forms, (2) standard responses, and (3) mail-merge functions.

Memoranda, notices, and other communications are often circulated on a standard form. If this form is created and saved using the word-processing program, it can easily be recalled and filled-in with appropriate information. Some word-processing programs allow for these forms to be saved as computer "macros," which can be recalled with only a keystroke. Thus, a memorandum form can be displayed on the screen by holding down one key (usually shift, control, or altmode key) and typing a single letter.

Fill-in forms can be created in the same way so that the individual using the word processing form simply "fills in the blanks," often with instructions displayed on the screen. Since the form does not have to be typed, the content can be personalized for the individual receiving the communication without a loss of time. In a library where there is a local area network, such forms can be stored in the network file server and are available "on call" to all users of the system without taking up space on the individual workstation disk(s).

Standard responses or information results from a study of what the library says to its publics when asked the same questions. Often libraries respond to individuals and to government agencies with the same information about library policies, descriptions of projects, and recent evaluations of services. Any library management group that has completed a grant request knows about the so called "boilerplate" information that must be supplied about the library, the staff, the personnel policies of the larger agency of which the library is a part, and the community in which the library operates. Any time the management staff identifies such information, it should be stored routinely as a disk file that can be called up by the word-processing program. If the library is using one kind of word-processing-application program, such files will automatically be available to anyone using the word-processing program simply by moving the file to the appropriate disk. If there is a local area network, such files can be stored in a single file-server subdirectory and will be available to everyone on the system.

Mail-merge programs (or simply, merge programs) allow for information from one file to be merged into the format of another file. One file contains "fields" of information; the other file contains instructions about which of those fields are to appear where in the final document. These programs allow for the same file of information to be used to create mailing labels, and name and address information in letters, telephone lists, and other lists.

For example, in one school-system media office, there is a file of records containing the following fields:

(1) media specialist's name
(2) school name
(3) principal's name
(4) school telephone number
(5) media specialist's home telephone number
(6) media specialist's home address

This file is used with at least four others: (1) a file that takes fields 1 and 2 to create courier-mailing labels for media specialists at school, (2) a file that takes fields 2 and 3 to create courier-mailing labels for school principals, (3) a file that takes fields 1 and 6 to create an envelope file for mailing information to media specialists' homes when school is not in session, and (4) a file that takes fields 1 and 5 to generate a telephone list of media specialists.

The library management staff will determine what information is used about a group of people (the library board, the library volunteer group, contacts in other community agencies, etc.) and then creates a file containing all of that information in separate fields. Since most word-processing-mailmerge programs allow for sorting of this information on the basis of fields, such lists are usually created with the person's last name and first name and the ZIP code in separate fields. Such an arrangement allows for sorting people into an alphabetical list by last names *and* putting the individual's name in regular order in a letter or list. Bulk-mailing regulations require ZIP code sorting, so that ability to sort a file by ZIP code, placing like ZIP codes together, is a great time saver. When the envelopes or labels are printed, they are in ZIP code order.

Another valuable part of word-processing programs is the ability to search for specific information in a file. The *search* command is typed, what is being searched-for is typed on the screen, and the program scans the file, character-by-character, looking for the first occurrence of those characters requested in the search. Such a function allows the user to move quickly to a remembered place in the file. When *search* is combined with *replace*, the user can search for a set of characters and replace them with another set.

Such a function is most useful when the original document is typed with short abbreviations for longer phrases.

For example, the author uses the character string, "UNCG" for the name of his university. After the draft is edited, search and replace are used to search for occurrences of "UNCG" and replace them with "The University of North Carolina at Greensboro." There is a tremendous saving of key strokes. Currently available word-processing programs also allow for indexing of every word in a file. Such an index can be used to determine words used most frequently in writing. I have developed two- to three-letter acronyms for about 50 words and phrases; many people have developed a whole series of such shorthand-typing character sets that can then be replaced in the final document.

An increasing number of program publishers are providing additional assistance for the written-communications process. Such assistance began with simple spell-checkers, where the text in the computer memory (or a single word) could be compared with a dictionary of correctly spelled words and the user could choose whether or not to replace that word with the displayed spelling. Personal dictionaries of often-used phrases, names, and acronyms could be included in the spell-check program so that the program would not reject those items as misspelled words.

These dictionary files have become larger and larger, and more and more specialized. It is possible to purchase a dictionary of technical, legal or medical terms for spell-checking. Programs have also added definitions and thesaurus-type functions, so that you can not only check the spelling, but also see a brief definition or select other synonyns or antonyms of the specified word. Other software publishers have issued special style- and grammar-checking programs that can be integrated into a word-processing-applications program. Examples of such programs include:

Correct Grammar by Lifetree Software, Inc., 33 New Montgomery Street, #1260, San Francisco, CA 94105
> Flags mistakes in grammar, style, punctuation, usage. Makes correction-suggestions and allows for the user to turn off specific rules as personal style dictates.

Right Writer by RightSoft, Inc., 4545 Samuel Street, Sarasota, FL 34233–9912
> Intended as an aid for business and technical writing. Uses over four thousand rules to analyze text of files produced by most word-processing programs. Provides a summary analysis at the end of a copy of the file.

Grammatik IV by Reference Software International, 330 Townsend Street, Suite 123, San Francisco, CA 94107

Grammar, syntax, sentence structure, and style analysis are provided immediately with on-screen feedback, and the user can make immediate changes.

Readability Program by Scandinavian PC Systems, 51 Monroe Street, Suite 707A, Rockville, MD 20850.

Provides a revised readability program that analyzes text in terms of average number of words per sentence and average number of long words per sentence in text. Selects sentences that fall outside readability limits and allows for reediting.

These rule-driven programs can be applied to a document file to check readability, level of difficulty, common grammar errors, strength (use of active, not passive voice), sentence and paragraph length, and the use of jargon.

Programs that interact with word-processing programs reach a pinnacle with the introduction of CD-ROM sets like Microsoft Corporation's *Bookshelf*, which contains the *American Heritage Dictionary*, *Roget's II: Electronic Thesaurus*, the *World Almanac and Book of Facts*, *Bartlett's Familiar Quotations*, the *Chicago Manual of Style*, and the *Houghton Mifflin Spelling Verifier and Corrector*. In addition, there is a file of forms and letters, a ZIP code directory, a grammar checker and a file of business information sources. A whole set of writing reference tools becomes available from *inside* word-processing-applications programs. While the user is typing a document, he or she may access any of these tools and import information into the current document. In local area networks, the CD-ROM device and the *Bookshelf* would be mounted with the file server and accessible to all users of the network.

Obviously, the ability to store legal materials, medical information, and other large reference tools like census data on CD-ROM will continue to develop and grow, influencing not only how library management handles text communication, but also what public services are offered to library patrons. One can even imagine the development of "library-specific" information in CD-ROM format, which would contain forms, letters, policy materials, library law, etc.

Library management staff wanting maximum benefit from word-processing systems will need to use one, common word-processing-application program. One cannot move word-processing format and controls from one applications package to another unless a translation package is used. Almost all of the current word-processing packages strive to show on the screen how the a page will look when printed. This "what-you-see-is-what-you-get" application means that a variety of special control characters are used to turn on and off underlining, boldface, and font-size applications. In addition, most of these programs also include information about the layout of pages (margins, spacing, etc.) that is not displayed on the screen. For example, in *WordPerfect* all the control characters and format information (including footnotes and indexing) are normally invisible. The user can turn on a screen that shows these functions, but the designers have been careful to design a screen that shows how the final copy will appear. All these control characters are unique to each word-processing package. This uniqueness means that importing word-processing files from one package to another is not simply copying the file. A file of only the text may be created and copied, but this file will not have page or line formatting or any of the special characters that control font size, underlining, bold, etc. A translation program can be used to change control characters from one system to another. Examples of such programs include:

Cross-Works, by Softspoken, Box 97623, Raleigh, NC 27624
Provides exchange between Appleworks and MS-Dos–type programs including: *Appleworks Wordprocessing* to and from *WordPerfect, Appleworks Spreadsheet* to and from Lotus *1–2–3, Appleworks Database* to and from *dBase III, IV.*

Software Bridge, Systems Compatibility Corporation, 401 N. Wabash, Suite 600, Chicago, IL 60611
A general conversion program for word-processing packages. They also offer specific, integrated packages for major word-processing programs which allow conversion to and from a specific application program to other word processing applications—*Star Exchange* for *WordStar, Perfect Exchange* for *WordPerfect.*

Considering the time such translation takes, and the necessity to clean up these files for use in the other word-processing package, a much better decision would be to all use the same word-processing package and, when a change is necessary, to upgrade with a compatible package.

Electronic Mail

Before leaving the topics of text communication and formatting in library management, some mention should be made of electronic mail (E-mail). Electronic mail provides the library with the ability to distribute information in electronic form within and among libraries. For example, if a school-library media supervisor wants to share a weekly update with all of the school-library media specialists, a wide area network will allow for the sending of that weekly update to each media center's "mailbox." Within a single library building, members of the staff can send each other information, and the privacy of that information can be secured. Some systems allow for an acknowledgement of the receipt of a message to be recorded for the sender. So, when a message is read, the receipt is recorded on the system.

General staff announcements can be "mailed" to everyone's mailbox. Committees working on documents can share drafts through the E-mail system. Several software vendors have products that allow comments and additions to be made to an original text without disturbing the original. A far simpler solution lies in bracketing the comment or corrections by each individual and moving the text to the next mailbox. Thus when one staff member receives a draft, he makes comments on that draft starting and ending with a line of ˆ ˆ ˆ ˆ ˆ ˆ ˆ ˆ or other symbols so that the comments stand out from the original text. It is also possible to create columns for comments using the later editions of *WordPerfect* or *WordStar*. Electronic mail (like other local area network features) works only as well as the managers who use it.

If the top library management uses electronic mail rather than memos or notes, the rest of the staff will be encouraged to do the same. Library managers will find they need to say, "Get back to me on E-mail" a number of times. Electronic mail usually includes a calendar function that can be used to schedule library events and present notices of outside meetings of interest. Such calendar functions can also be used for work scheduling of the library staff. While electronic calendars are excellent for the library's top management, they will not replace the pocket calendars of most staff members. The staff does not take the workstation to lunch, meetings, or conferences. Remembering to record information when returning to the library is difficult. However, a master calendar of the library can be maintained in this way.

Planning, Evaluation, and Budgeting

Planning, evaluation, and budget analysis become much easier with the use of workstation-based spreadsheet applications. Spreadsheet software ranges from very simple "flat" spreadsheet development tools, which allow for formula calculations related to specific cells (or row and columns), to highly complex spreadsheet software, which allows for the development of special macro instructions so that the person using the spreadsheet receives instructions about what data to enter. Many of the more complex spreadsheets allow for the development of graphic presentation of the numerical data in several forms—bars, pie charts, etc. Such graphic representations are useful in reports and other documents where masses of numbers simply confuse both the presenter and the audience.

Spreadsheet application programs are basically electronic ledger sheets. These programs help the library manager turn a mass of data into useful information for decision making. As such, they require the same care with numbers and formulas as manual accounting. It is still true that errors in numbers or calculations give false results; the spreadsheet program allows for such errors to multiply at a great rate. The library management staff will need to study their spreadsheet results to see if they "make sense."

Library managers have always had to deal with counting of things and the resultant numbers. In a workstation or a local area network, the computer's capacity to generate reams of numbers on paper can be overwhelming. Spreadsheet programs allow for the creation of data-based information where the results of calculating one set of numbers against another can be easily seen. They also allow for comparing one library with others in very specific areas.

For example, the hypothetical public library of Norlina County can compare the circulation statistics of its various branches as shown in Table 3.

In this example formulas have been entered in the columns labeled INCR (DECR), %INCR(DECR) so that the following questions can be asked about each branch: (1) how much did circulation increase or decrease? (2) what was the percentage of that change? Even better comparisons could be made if circulation data were available for more years or circulation changes were compared with funds spent on staff and materials or with other factors. The capacity to comparatively aggregate data over time and in different locations, and compare it in meaningful ways, can be very useful in the library-management decision-making process. Since this data is now entered

Table 3.
Comparison of Libraries' Circulation Statistics

BRANCH	YR-1986	YR-1987	INCR/ (DECR)	%INCR/ (DECR)	PROJECTED YR-1988	INCR/ (DECR)	%INCR/ (DECR)
MARSHALL	290,877	292,987	2,110	.72	298,520	5,533	1.89
W. MARSHALL	34,765	35,176	411	1.17	37,220	2,044	5.81
BAXTER	7,954	7,122	(832)	(11.68)	6,250	(872)	(12.24)
THURGOOD	108,920	111,894	2,974	2.66	130,400	18,506	16.54
BOOKMOBILE	4,899	5,260	361	6.86	5,950	690	13.12
EXTENSION	1,379	1,464	85	5.81	1,575	111	7.58
TOTAL	448,794	453,903	5,109	1.13	479,915	26,012	5.73

into the spreadsheet, additional columns for other data or formulas can simply be inserted. The raw circulation numbers for each branch do not tell the library manager much in isolation; gathered together across time and among branches, the numbers become meaningful.

Even without statistical techniques, it is easy to see that the Baxter Branch is in difficulty. Library management can then seek out the causes of that difficulty: hours of operation, population decline, population characteristics, collection characteristics, geographic location, competing information sources.

Internal comparative data is useful, but library managers often want to know about how their libraries compare with other libraries. Since multiple variables influence library operations, the library manager needs to compare his or her library with libraries that are similar in many ways. The Public Library Association now publishes an annual *Public Library Data Service Statistical Report* (published annually), which groups libraries by population size, shows sources of income, salary, and other budget details, and gives some operating-expenditure measures: expenditures per capita, salaries as a percentage of expenditures, materials as a percentage of expenditures, and material expenditures per capita. If the public library of Norlina County is placed in the context of libraries serving areas of similar population size, we get a table like that shown in Table 4.

Other useful comparisons could be made on the basis of budget, staff size, etc., not population. Spreadsheet programs allow for "snapshot comparisons."

Perhaps the most powerful aspect of spreadsheet software is the ability to use the software to develop "what-if" situations related to changes in various parts of the library budget. When a library is developing a budget presentation it becomes important to study the alternatives for either a budget increase or decrease. In my area, many agencies are routinely asked to prepare budget requests reflecting increases and decreases at the same time. When a library management team has done basic cost analysis of the various cost centers, as is suggested by Rosenburg in his *Costfinding for Public Libraries* (1985), then the team can use a spreadsheet model to determine the impact of specific line-item changes in the budget on various library operations. Decisions related to the costs of various equipment or service contracts can also be simulated in the same way. Any type of simple statistical analysis can be created on a workstation spreadsheet. Models of "templates" of various budget, reporting, and statistical applications are available.

While many library managers are already using spreadsheets, it is important to stress the utility and ease of such applications programs for *every* library manager. Sources for further readings on spreadsheet applications for library management appear at the end of this chapter.

Table 4.
Statistical Comparison of Libraries of Similar Size

POPULATION	LIBRARY	TOTAL INCOME	MATERIALS EXPENDITURE	OTHER	TOTAL	EXPENDITURES PER CAPITA	MATERIALS AS % OF EXPEND	MATERIALS $ PER CAPITA
140000	CLERMONT,OH	2374547.00	455526.00	1341491.00	1797017.00	12.84	25.35	3.25
139712	ROCKFORD,IL	3243365.00	446529.00	1390944.00	1837473.00	13.15	24.30	3.20
138400	JACKSON CTY,OR	1511778.00	201684.00	279128.00	480812.00	3.47	41.95	1.46
137970	PATERSON FREE,NJ	1370132.00	172924.00	276790.00	449714.00	3.26	38.45	1.25
137920	MARIN CTY,CA	2987650.00	70809.00	115511.00	186320.00	1.35	38.00	.51
137473	TUSCALOOSA,AL	1301183.00	70809.00	115511.00	186320.00	1.36	38.00	.52
135599	SAINT CLAIR CTY,MI	1430478.00	101471.00	426264.00	527735.00	3.88	19.23	.75
135282	RAPIDES PARISH,LA	1166017.00	166928.00	241758.00	408686.00	3.02	40.85	1.23
135200	HARTFORD,CT	4093930.00	375700.00	552460.00	928160.00	6.87	40.48	2.78
135069	COLLIER CTY,FL	1021333.00	161634.00	188608.00	350242.00	2.59	46.15	1.20
134659	MONROE CTY,MI	2521681.00	480966.00	372397.00	853363.00	6.34	56.36	3.57
134655	YORK,ON	2695366.00	247960.00	713960.00	961920.00	7.14	25.78	1.84
134532	DANIEL BOONE,MT	1749741.00	276162.00	454534.00	730696.00	5.43	37.79	2.05
133800	SHASTA CTY,CA	964808.00	92610.00	191615.00	284225.00	2.12	32.58	.69
133235	ANDERSON CTY,SC	1022866.00	167969.00	246439.00	414408.00	3.11	40.53	1.26
133000	BIBLIOTHEQUE MUN.,PR	1333314.00	198387.00	250573.00	448960.00	3.38	44.19	1.49
132329	CAPE BRETON,NS	742914.00	146231.00	127907.00	274138.00	2.07	53.34	1.11
130800	PASADENA,CA	4769388.00	473319.00	1342216.00	1815535.00	13.88	26.07	3.62
130719	PUNKIN CTY,NC	749388.00	116000.00	32250.00	148250.00	1.13	78.25	.89
130058	KENTON CTY,KY	1395722.00	236950.00	410114.00	647064.00	4.98	36.62	1.82
130000	GLENDALE,AZ	2902867.00	272000.00	2883000.00	3115000.00	24.27	8.62	2.09
129315	OSHWAWA,ON	2223292.00	287308.00	500348.00	787656.00	6.09	36.48	2.22

Online catalog systems and integrated library systems are local area networks configured to present information about the library collection to the library's public. These systems also generate information useful for library management. Although early online catalog systems did not have integral statistical-generating capabilities, many current online catalog systems and integrated systems can be programmed to create informative reports such as exception reports ("display all cases outside of a certain range"), reports on parts of the system not typically generated ("what is the volume of activity in X subsystem?"), and longitudinal reports ("what do the numbers show over a period of years?"). Collection-management information (having what people need in the collection, based on an analysis of what they have requested) can be gathered easily from the circulation module of any integrated library system.

The online catalog system provides a means of actually studying the use of the catalog by the library's public and making decisions about how the system can be improved to be more helpful. Transaction logs allow study of an individual patron's activity (without knowing who that patron is), activities of various terminals (which locations are used most heavily?), and how long it takes for people to find what they need or give up. A careful management analysis of transaction logs can reveal where the public is having difficulty with the system and allow the management to consider changes in displays, equipment, or search-software options.

Management analysis of online catalog systems is not limited to a study of transaction logs. Other analyses can include: (1) response-time measures—how long does it take the system to respond to x? (2) capacity analysis—how much of our existing resources are being used by the system when it operates at various levels? (3) longitudinal studies of system performance—is the system continuing to perform at an acceptable level? Longitudinal studies are only possible if the library management staff established base-line performance operating data.

Management staff can also study various data generated by the online system to determine ways in which the system can be "tuned" or refined for better use. Such study should include not only the public use of the online catalog system, but also the variety of library staff uses of that system. If the circulation or reference staff is waiting an unreasonable time for specific system responses, the library's public suffers. Readers wanting more information on computer-based library management information systems are referred to the reading list at the end of this chapter.

Communication and Public Relations

If the library management group is using text processing and sophisicated spreadsheet programs, a wide variety of presentation materials becomes available. In these situations, integrated applications software—which allows for text, graphs, and spreadsheet numbers to be placed in the same document—will be useful. Such integrated software is available for every major microcomputer made. The ability to "cut and paste" information from databases, spreadsheets, and text processors into one document simplifies the creation of reports and—combined with desktop publishing software—can be used to create very professional-appearing publications for the library's public. Of course, high-quality publication for a public that is not there, or a public that is not interested, is irrelevant to the library. Professional publication does not replace careful market analysis by the library management.

Desktop publishing applications programs include a number of "layout" functions, including the ability to change the size of type as well as select from a variety of saved type fonts. The position of text on a page in relationship to graphics can easily be controlled, and a variety of useful column functions is usually included. An increasing number of graphic-illustrations packages are available for insertion into desktop publishing programs. The user merely selects the graphic and inserts it in the appropriate place in the text. Most graphics software for use with desktop publishing allows for changing the size of illustration, rotating it, creating negative images, and inserting text into the illustration itself. Many desktop publishing applications can be operated using the mouse devices now commonly found with personal computers. Many people find this "point and click" system very easy to use—especially those who have not had a lot of keyboarding experience.

The ability to add graphics to text materials has been enhanced by a variety of scanning devices, which digitize pictures on paper, creating disk files that can then be imported into the desktop publishing application and modified for use. Scanning devices range from hand-held scanners (two hundred to three hundred dollars) to page-size scanners (one thousand to two thousand dollars). If a library is doing a great deal of in-house publication, desktop publishing programs (and related graphics programs) can be used to create professional-looking flyers, newsletters, etc.

A word of warning: once a library management groups starts down the path of desktop publishing, the need for professional-looking brochures, bookmarks, signs, bibliographies, annual reports, and the like grows dramatically. Good, easy-to-use desktop software is addictive: the amount of materials needed will grow to take all of the time of some staff members if that is allowed to happen. Given the right skills in the staff, the appropriate software, and excellent printing capability (usually a laser printer), the library staff can replace the outside printer and often duplicate the quality.

The problem here is a true estimate of costs. The library staff can do all of these things in more and more sophisticated ways. However, library "runs" of printed items are usually not very large, so staff puts a great deal of time into a small-scale production, often creating (or buying disks of) graphics and logos as well as carefully laying out pages and managing formats for double, triple, and quadruple folds. Commercial copying and printing companies are also making use of the developing desktop publishing software and equipment. Often they can provide better equipment, better software, more routine graphics, and higher-quality layouts at a lower cost to the library. For some staff, desktop publishing will become a creative endeavor, but the library management should always do a careful cost-benefit analysis of when to create in house and when to go outside.

Since outside costs are falling radically and special-effects software is increasingly available, the cost analysis will need to be repeated regularly. It takes a large volume of a variety of printed materials to justify staff time, training, and equipment maintenance.

Conclusion

The library manager's workstation needs to be designed so that it can truly function as a *work* station that is easy for the manager to use in supervising, planning, and evaluating the work of the library. Poorly designed workstations are not used, and managers continue to work as they have in the past. In a local area network environment, the library manager's workstation should be connected to other units on the network so that the ease of access to relevant and useful information is increased. As in all other areas, the manager needs to guard against doing work that others can do. The local area network should be configured so that electronic delegation is possible: do the draft, let the secretary make it look professional; take the notes, have someone else on the network make them into minutes.

Further Reading

Library Spreadsheets

Auld, L. W. S. 1986. *Electronic spreadsheets for libraries.* Phoenix, Ariz.: Oryx Press.

Bichteler, J., et al. 1986. Role of computers in sci-tech libraries. *Science and Technology Libraries* 6 (Summer) 1–145.

Bergin, R. 1986. Microcomputer software use in libraries. *Library Software Review* 5 (November–December): 332–36.

Clark, P. M. Accounting as evaluation, as reporting: The use of online accounting systems. *Drexel Library Quarterly* 21 (Summer): 61–74.
———. 1985. *Microcomputer spreadsheet models for libraries: Preparing documents, budgets, and statistical reports.* Chicago: American Library Association.

Library Management Decision-Information Systems

Boland, R. J., Jr. 1982. Tutorial on management information systems. *In Proceedings: Library automation as a source of management information, clinic on library applications of data processing.* Urbana, Ill.: University of Illinois, Graduate School of Library and Information Science, 10–26.
Cortez, E. M. 1983. Library automation and management information systems. *Journal of Library Automation* 4 (Fall): 21–33.
Gordon, K. L. 1988. The UNIX/XENIX advantage: Applications in libraries. *Library Software Review* 7 (January–February): 20–21.
Hawks, C. P. 1988. Management information gleaned from automated library systems. *Information Technology and Libraries* 7 (2): 124–30.
———. 1986. The Geac acquisition system as a source of management information. *Library Acquisitions: Theory and Practice* 10(4): 245–53.
Herceg, J. D. 1986. Acquisition management information on a shoestring. *Small Computers in Libraries* 6(8): 20–28.
Hoehl, S. B. 1988. Local area networks: Effective tools for special libraries *Online* 12 (September): 64–68.
Kaske, N. A. 1988. A comparative study of subject searching in an OPAC among branch libraries of a university library system. *Information Technology and Libraries* 7 (December): 359–72.
Lynch, C. A. 1988. Response time measurement and performance analysis in public access information retrieval systems. *Information Technology and Libraries* 7 (June): 177–83.
Main, L. 1987. Decision support with decision-modeling software. *Library Software Review* 6 (May–June): 128–33.
Moskowitz, M. 1985. The collection manager's micro. *Technicalities* 5 (March): 11–14.
Perry-Holmes, C. Lotus *1-2-3* and decision support: Allocating the monograph budget. *Library Software Review* 4 (July–August): 205–13.
Raymond, C., and Anderson, C. 1987. Local area networks: Reaping the benefits. *Wilson Library Bulletin* 62 (November): 21–24.
Tague, J. 1979. Computer potential for management information. *Canadian Library Journal* 36 (October): 268–70.

4

Public Access to Workstations and the Local Area Network

The computing industry is driven by the corporate and government markets and not by the library market. In this larger arena libraries have a relatively small place. Libraries, or those who would sell to libraries, will take technology created by others and adapt it for their own purposes.
[Flower, 1988, p. 24]

The library's public will typically have access to two types of workstations and local area networks: (1) the library's own workstations and network in public-access reference services, circulation services, and online catalogs, and (2) workstations and local area networks dedicated to public-access uses not related to library services. This chapter discusses the development and management of both types of public-access systems.

Public Workstations

Workstations used by the library's public require special planning. The staff cannot assume that the public has had training or experience with personal computers or related software. The library staff needs to consider specific issues related to public-access microcomputers: (1) establishing the goals of public access workstation areas, (2) determining management responsibility, (3) selecting sites and layouts for workstation areas, (3) selecting equipment and providing maintenance, (4) selecting and securing applications programs, 5) estimating the demands placed on staff and equipment, and (6) securing library files and equipment. Each of these issues is discussed below.

Goals of Operation

Before offering access to its public, any library must be very clear about the goals of that operation. Does the library intend that workstations will be

67

used only for library-related activities? Does the library support other types of computer activities? How do the goals and objectives of the public-access workstation area fit into the goals and objectives of the overall library program? Because the library staff is clear about the goals of the program does not mean the library's users will share those goals. Once the goals of the program are clear, they will need to be publicized among the library users, and policies will need to be created to deal with computer uses in conflict with the goals. It is critical that the library's goals and objectives guide the technology, *not* the technology guide the library's operations.

Responsibility

Often libraries are part of larger institutions which have a stake in public-access workstation operations. For example, the academic library may be the *site* of a public-access area, but the academic departments and the computer center of the campus will also have an interest in the operation. Even when public access is limited to public-access online catalogs, the responsibility for operation, maintenance, and upgrading must be clear. Cimbala (1985) discusses the problems relating to sharing management of the center with other units. These include:

who determines the schedule of the public-access facility?
who is responsible for the hiring and supervision of staff for the area?
who determines what applications software is available?
who is ultimately responsible for dealing with policy issues?

All of these factors need to be discussed and responsibilities clarified. Remember that what no one is responsible for is always what happens. Shared management responsibilities can work, but only if there are good communications, clear policy, and an efficient way to deal with problems as they emerge.

Site and Layout

Libraries are not usually in a situation where there is a lot of unused space available for development. Library staff members should pay particular attention to the ergonomics of the site including: light, noise, and user comfort (see chapter 6 of this book on ergonomic issues). If the public use of the workstation is very short-term, workstations can be placed so that individuals can use them while standing. Any extended use of workstations (as in word processing or bibliographic instruction) will need to provide some form of adjustable seating for the user.

Where several workstations are in proximity, and printing capabilities are provided, care should be taken to limit the noise of several machines and printers. Placement of machines in carrel-type enclosures can be helpful. Acoustic covers for printers will also help. If the library can afford to offer laser printers to their users, much of the noise factor is eliminated. In some public areas, the only solution may be printers that operate by heat transfer and are virtually silent. A more complete discussion of the ergonomics of workstations will be found in chapter 6.

Normally the establishment of public-access workstation areas involves a considerable investment of money. The library staff will need to develop security procedures for the facility, the equipment, and the software. A number of companies offer tie-down mechanisms, which allow for securing computer equipment to tables or carrels. There is also the option of a locking cabinet that encloses the whole machine and printer. Software security and copyright compliance are more difficult. In situations where the public access online catalog can also be used to access remote databases— the "article-level" access now being developed in some research and academic libraries—copyright compliance issues become more difficult. One printed copy of a citation, an abstract, or a full-text article may be all right, but what if the system allows the user to download that information onto a personal floppy disk or workstation? The library staff must be clear about licensing agreements and who is liable.

If the workstation is part of a local area network, the applications programs can be loaded on the file server, and the public has access to the use of the program but not to the application program disks. If floppy disks of programs are made available for checkout and use, some procedure for getting them returned and checking the operating condition of the disks will need to be established.

A good part of the security problem (as well as the user-assistance problem) can be solved by locating the workstation area in proximity to staff locations so that staff can observe, supervise, and assist the users. Unattended workstation areas tend to collect security problems including abuse of equipment and software, theft, and illegal copying. A basic rule of location is, "never place the workstation area where it can be seen from outside the building." (Dewey, 1984, p. 52)

Some of the abuse of public-access systems results from "hacking" by individuals who know how to get into the management areas of disks, computers, and local area networks and create annoying messages, destroy files, and generally cause difficulty. Many hackers' activities are harmless; however, some hackers leave viruses on the computer hard disk or on floppy disks they have overwritten. Library staff will need to monitor their systems for these possibilities. Several companies have produced antivirus programs that prevent viruses from being loaded. In some cases, the public may need to be restricted to using applications-programs disks that belong to the library.

Libraries may have electrical problems with any site chosen because of the age of the library facility. Electrical issues include: adequate wiring and grounding, appropriate placement of outlets, and containment of wires and cables. In some situations, the workstation site will require rewiring because either the electrical system will not take the additional workstation electrical equipment, or turning on equipment in other areas of the library causes line fluctuation or power outages.

Many ideal sites do not have adequate grounded electrical outlets. It is tempting to run extension boxes around the floor and under workstation tables. It may be far better to have an electrician add additional outlets around the wall (in metal casings) or provide wiring in drop poles near work stations. Whenever possible, wiring should not be run across the floor (even in molded floor channels). Care should be taken to meet the electrical and building code of the jurisdiction in which the library operates. Such rerouting of electrical wires will add to the expense of setting up the workstation site. It is also important to remember that adding outlets does not increase the electrical power available.

Equipment

Public access workstations are selected on the basis of user needs. If the public identifies its needs as database management, spreadsheets, and text processing, computers that follow the general MS-DOS pattern of operation will have more general appeal. If graphs, color graphics, or desktop publishing are the major concerns, the APPLE IIGS and Macintosh may be the solution.

As was mentioned in chapter 1, the Macintosh computer, with its mouse and desktop publishing software, has become very popular in situations where enhanced text and graphic capabilities are needed. The ability to design and produce high-quality brochures, bookmarks, and posters needs to be considered. For the library's public, these distinctions of brands of equipment are becoming less important as the major companies develop equipment and software that duplicate each other's capabilities. For example, *WordPerfect 5.0* has considerable font and graphics capabilities and *WordStar 5.0* has a program capacity to deal with graphics. The more graphic- and color-oriented the user population is, the more carefully printers and monitors will have to be selected. Many graphics programs now demand an extended graphics (EGA) monitor (or even a VGA monitor and adapter). Color graphics on the screen that are printed out in tones of black, white, and gray, tend to lose a lot in printing.

If graphics capabilities are essential, the library staff should explore those text processors that treat all information as a graphic form (rather than text being treated as ASCII code). Before purchasing any desktop publishing equipment or software, the staff should use it. Paying for a training session at a community college or commercial firm is preferable to purchasing graphic-capacity equipment and software and then finding it very difficult to use.

Curtis (1988) reviews the requirements of scholarly library users and offers some tentative conclusions:

libraries will use standard microcomputer hardware rather than proprietary equipment

scholars will increasingly demand special character sets and character-generating capabilities

scholars will want graphics capabilities: storage and retrieval and probably communication over distance

information access, as seen in the library workstation connected to various bibliographic and full-text sources, will become increasing popular in other scholarly settings.

While discussing graphic text, the library staff should be careful to analyze the actual uses of text materials in the library environment. Library staff and publics create an amazing volume of text that does not require any special fonts, graphics, or special layouts. Support staff will become extremely frustrated with highly technical desktop publishing layout systems if the bulk of their work is normal text output. If library staff has access to dot-matrix or laser printers that can take character-oriented text and create different text sizes and fonts, the need for special desktop publishing software is greatly reduced.

Along with the quality and type of textual materials that will be processed, the library staff needs to consider how that text will be made into hard copy. Printers abound in a variety of dot-matrix, daisywheel and laser forms. There is no question that the $1,500 laser printer (often enhanced with special font cartridges) produces excellent-quality print, which can be reproduced with professional-level results. Still, sending memoranda, inventory lists, and drafts by laser printer seems excessive and very slow. In larger operations, the library is likely to tie one very good laser printer into a local area network and establish several sites where "draft-quality" printout can be produced at high speed with dot-matrix equipment.

Although workstations and other PC configurations have been hailed as the beginning of a paperless society, often the most common products of the public-access workstation area are printed documents—with the attendant problems of printer jams, complaints about print quality, and noise. Considerable eating up of ribbons and wasted paper occurs in any text-processing situation. However, if public access workstations are used to learn text processing, or to develop desktop publishing skills, the amount of waste will increase significantly.

Staff needs to think through how they will respond to the connectivity issue when their public users want to transfer one file into another applications program, or to a different brand of machine. Responses can range from, "we don't offer that service" to "call up the transfer program and follow the directions on the menu to get a usable copy of your program." Libraries offering one kind of workstation and one set of software can avoid many problems, but they will still have to deal with the individual who brings in files on a disk that must be converted in order to operate on the library's system.

Programs: Selection and Security

Intner (1988) sees the most important question asked about library software collections to be: "who will use the collection?" A careful selection of software is not enough; the library staff will need to analyze the present and potential users of that software application.

If public-access workstations are on a local area network system, applications software must be selected that can be loaded on a hard disk and utilized in the network. Some applications and instructional software cannot legally be copied onto a hard disk, or the library staff will not be able to get permission to make such copies. An increasing amount of applications software is available for network applications. A list of sources of library applications programs is found at the end of this chapter.

Libraries develop different ways of dealing with applications programs and documentation. For example, Frazer Library of the State University of New York at Geneseo handles applications software as part of the reserve book collection (MacLean, 1988). The library supplies not only software, but also manuals and related materials, which can be checked out at the reserve desk. A database applications package is used to maintain printed lists of available software and documentation.

Libraries will also need policy to deal with copyright of application programs. Copyright issues are related to the appropriate legal use of intellectual property covered by the United States Copyright Law. Title 17 of the United States Code was extensively revised in 1976 (P. L. 94-553). The revision established the National Commission on New Technological Uses of Copyrighted Works (CONTU). Congress amended the law in 1980 on the basis of the commission's recommendations.

McKirdy (1988) provides a summary of the sections of the 1976 Copyright Act and reviews a number of court cases involving infringement of copyright in areas of software programs, including cases where the "look and feel" of programs was protected. For librarians, major issues exist in the areas of:

> the ability (or inability) to copyright a cooperatively developed database, such as OCLC, which would impact the ability to download data and later utilize that data in printed or database form
>
> the ownership of applications programs or equipment configurations developed by library staff, which are not clearly a part of their regularly assigned tasks
>
> the copying of applications programs for other-than-archival purposes (see Stanek, 1986)

Practical problems include how a program is to be protected from misuse in a network situation. Some vendors of applications software offer site licenses for special programs packages. Others sell "packs" or software at a reduced rate per copy.

Each library needs written policy related to the use of software. That policy should point out copyright-law provisions and those activities that are illegal. Some libraries have potential users of the software sign a copyright-policy statement prior to utilizing the software. Duke and Hirshon (1986), the Association of Research Libraries (1985), and the Association of Data Processing Service Organizations (1985) provide guidelines on such policies.

Demands on Staff and Equipment

The library's patrons can demand a great deal of staff attention as they begin to use workstations and local area networks. People starting to use any type of computer are often puzzled by what they see on the screen. They cannot tell (1) where they are in the program, or (2) how to get from where they are to the next step. Staff time is needed to assist people in learning to operate the system and to evaluate the system so that it can be changed and made more understandable.

Camardo (1988, p. 33) notes that the demand for individual instruction (or assistance) means that the library will find: (1) increased amounts of staff time are devoted to individual instruction, and (2) the need for trained staff assistants increases. Library managers should note the essential difference between staff training and public training: the public does not have to tolerate bad training—in terms of quality of instruction, amount of time needed to learn an application, or bad attitudes on the part of staff. The public will simply go elsewhere, or worse, try to use the systems and programs without any instruction, only to find the systems "can't be used."

Those interested in further reading on instruction of the library's public are referred to the reading list at the end of this chapter.

Even if a public-access workstation area is successful because of appropriate selection of hardware and applications, the demand for use for different needs will come into conflict. In academic settings, the public-access workstation area will be used for classroom-type instruction, even if originally intended for individual use. Eventually some type of scheduling system will need to be installed in many public-access workstation settings. The principle of "first come, first served" and the use of signup sheets become too unwieldy to manage.

In settings where group instruction takes place, the purchase of a projection device and the creation of a classroom with one workstation, applications software, and group display facilities may ease the pressure on the public-access workstations. Relatively inexpensive plasma display devices, which can be used with overhead projectors and workstations, are available. Examples include:

Boxlight, Boxlight Corporation, 448 Ignacio Boulevard, Suite 254, Novato, CA 94949

Data Display Multimode, Computer Accessories Corporation, 6610 Nancy Ridge Drive, San Diego, CA 92121 (also makes MAC Data Display for Macintosh machines)

MagnaByte, Telex Communications, Inc., 9600 Aldrich Avenue, South Minneapolis, MN 55420

Magnaview, Dukane, Audio Visual Division, 2900 Dukane Drive, St. Charles, IL 60174

Libraries creating public-access workstation areas will need to have clear policies related to the use (and potential abuse) of equipment, applications software, and staff. Policies should include statements on:

how people schedule access to the equipment

policies on food, drinking, and smoking (just say no)

responsibilities for paying (or not paying) for the use of peripheral devices like printers, plotters, laser output devices

copying of software (don't)

If a printer is going to be in a public-access area, where patrons can use the printer as part of a public-access system, the noise of the printer and its ability to withstand public abuse need to be taken into consideration. The way paper is fed into and removed from the printer must be very simple. In some settings, thermal printers may be the only alternative because of noise factors.

Specific Uses

Reference and Collection

Among the most basic public-access services of a library are reference and information services. For several decades, libraries have been using some form of computer link to access remote databases of bibliographic information. The use of such systems by library staff is gradually being replaced (or supplemented) by public use of the systems, as the library's patrons become more sophisticated and want to do the searching themselves (often from their own offices). Vendors who previously offered only online index, abstract, and full-text services now offer their products in CD-ROM form with the necessary workstations to operate these systems.

Currently there are problems in the area of applications software. While most vendors adhere to some form of the informal "High Sierra" standard, they develop programs to manipulate their CD-ROM and online systems in their own way. Often the way in which a workstation is configured must be changed for each of the different systems. When a CD from a different vendor is used, the system must be restarted. As the applications programs to operate CD-ROM devices as disk drives change, the particular vendor software may (or may not) require such an applications update. For example, my program on one CD-ROM index service requires software extensions dated after June 1989; another CD-ROM index cannot use the configuration of that system, and the user must restart the workstation with different configuration files. Imagine what happens when a public-services area has CD-ROM packages from seven or eight sources! One answer to this problem has been to mount the CD-ROM disks on a local area network and use advanced configuration/operations software. Libraries will need expert assistance to get local area network CD-ROM systems operating. There is still a need for applications software that will sense the particular format of CD-ROM files and provide both access to indexes of that file and also a search capability.

The H. W. Wilson Company began to offer its online/CD-ROM workstation on IBM PC/XT machines and later switched to an IBM PS/2 system when IBM dropped the PC series. Their newer systems provide VGA graphics and additional 3½-inch disk storage. Wilson now offers a local area network version of their software and CD-ROMs. Information Access Company's Infotrac II and the newer Infotrac Reference Center use their own software and videodisc-mounted databases. Their workstation package includes everything needed to set up a public-access reference station, including printers. The Infotrac Reference Center uses their workstation as a file server for up to eight workstations and provides access to online systems through a modem. This system can support up to eight CD-ROM drives and/or the same number of videodisc players. More information about CD-ROM use by the library's public will be found in the further reading list at the end of this chapter.

Changes in telephone tariffs since the breakup of AT&T have increased the costs of online reference services. Miller and Gratch (1989) describe the expanded range of activities now found in computerized reference services, pointing out that such activities include an enhanced role for the librarian as intermediary, a larger role for the end user, and problems of cost, instruction, standardization, space, and security that have yet to be solved.

In a few years, library users have come to expect some form of workstation-based reference service that will allow access to abstracts and indexes on a relatively current basis. They often confuse such services with full-document retrieval. A bewildering array of CD/ROM, online, and full-text systems exists. Artificial-intelligence software is being used to assist end users in developing and selecting search terms and search strategies, selecting databases, and doing the actual search.

Nelson (1988) notes the trend toward the development of "front-end" applications packages for similar remote-site database access. Several companies now offer bibliographic-searching "front ends," which deal with software protocols of the local equipment, the remote site system, and provide files for the storage of passwords and other messages essential to running the system.

Examples of this development are *Pro-Search* for DIALOG (Personal Bibliographic Software, Ann Arbor, Mich.) and *WILSEARCH* (H. W. Wilson Company). The user of such systems merely indicates the database to be searched, and the software deals with all of the "initial" transactions including dialing, connect protocols, and passwords. The user begins with searching, not remembering how to sign on. For example, OCLC provides the OCLC *LINK* service, which provides access to remote databases as well as the ability to download records and communicate with other users of the system. In addition, OCLC provides access to a large subset of the OCLC catalog through BRS. CD/ROM versions of various OCLC databases (or subsets of databases) are also available. Almost every vendor of online reference services now provides a CD/ROM (sometimes full-text) alternative.

CD-ROM databases will not replace online services. The traditional use of the workstation as what Futas (1988) calls a "front-end terminal" will continue so long as massive amounts of online information continue to be made available. That amount of information has increasingly come to mean full-text of articles and other materials, and may soon come to include online line-access to the graphics contained in those articles.

Full-text retrieval frees the patron (and the librarian) from consulting articles and books, and allows a browsing of sources while the user works in one place. Many large databases, such as the Bureau of Census database or various financial-information databases, can be manipulated by the user at the workstation, utilizing software provided by the vendor of the online bibliographic database. Whole reference works stored on CD-ROMs are now available. My favorites remain the complete *Oxford English Dictionary* with special retrieval software and detailed indexing, or the digitized maps of major areas based on census data.

Interlibrary-loan activities can also be handled by workstations and wide area networks so that materials can not only be located much faster, but also information can be transferred from one library to another by FAX machines. Many workstations will include FAX cards, which allow FAX transmissions to be captured to disk and edited with a local-applications word-processing package.

The bibliographic-instruction function of the library reference department can be aided by workstation installation. Dubin and Kuhner (1986) explore the use of microcomputers in library instruction. In libraries where a number of workstations are connected through a local area network, one option in bibliographic instruction is a series of instructional packages, mounted on the file server, which the reference department patron can use at his or her own pace. A hypermedia capability exists that allows for the combination of text instructions, graphics of available reference tools, and actual scanned pictures of the areas of the library facility being discussed. Touch-windows, like those that allow for interactive guide maps to shopping mall stores, could be used to guide the library's public to subject areas of the reference collection.

The use of workstations by reference-area patrons raises some specific questions:

(1) What safeguards are provided to protect the confidentiality of patron information activities?

If workstation activity is logged, and a record is kept of the patron's search activities on the system, that information needs to be secured in the same way that patrons' circulation records are secured from investigation by interested parties. Since the Federal Bureau of Investigation (as well as some members of the National Commission on Libraries and Information Science) have taken the view that citizens do not have a right to such privacy, the library staff will need to develop internal guidelines on the privacy of patron access to information, whether on CD-ROM or online. Keeping records of search activities by library staff and patrons is not only possible, but may actually assist the library in discovering how staff and patrons can use the systems more effectively. However, if such a record is kept, it should be secured, and patrons should be able to use the system without identifying themselves.

(2) What applications software should the library acquire?

The library staff cannot acquire all published reference and information software, or even that requested by library users. The library staff will need to utilize existing software-review resources in order to spend their software acquisition dollars wisely. Dewey (1988, p. 64) outlines a series of steps for software review and acquisitions:

(a) what is needed?
(b) how do we find the software that will do that job?
(c) of the available programs which is the best?
(d) will the software that does the job and appears to be the best work on our equipment?
  is more memory required?
  does the software require special cards or devices?
  is a different type of monitor required?

Sources of reviews include the popular computer press as well as many of the journals in library literature. A review article should tell the reader what equipment is necessary (amount of memory, special devices, etc.), indicate potential problems of understanding the documentation or screen directions, and list any special peripherals needed. The personal evaluation of the reviewer may not be as significant as the facts of the case. Where possible, reviews from the library field are most helpful. Dewey offers an excellent summary of journal titles in which reviews occur within the library field and in the popular computer field.

Intner (1988) spells out the following steps in developing a library software collection:

gather data about potential uses, potential users, available resources
develop goals and objectives for the collection in harmony with the overall materials-collection goals and objectives
develop a software-collection project schedule
designate responsible staff, and begin site preparation
develop policies on use of software and equipment
consult with appropriate staff on cataloging and circulation procedures
maintain ongoing consultation with end users of the software collection
develop policies on selection and acquisition of software in line with current selection and acquisition policies
build software-collection evaluation into the plan

The library staff needs to view the development of workstations and local area networks as regular parts of the library operation. In the same way, software-collection development should be integrated into the total library-collection-development and user-services operations. Workstation areas, public-access microcomputers, and related software should not be seen in isolation from the rest of the library.

(3) How should the library pay for online or CD-ROM reference services?

The old "fee or free" debate continues. No information that is collected, organized, and then disseminated is truly free. Somewhere, the labor for the efforts expended must be included in costs. Many libraries have provided free information services, which meant that the individual patron was not *directly* charged for any portion of the costs of reference-materials selection and acquisition, or for the time of the reference staff member. Such costs were hidden in the total operating budget of the library and paid for by the larger institution (as in academic libraries) or by state and local taxes (as in public libraries).

The costs of most CD-ROM and online bibliographic services are not so easy to hide. At the end of each online search, a cost summary is transmitted from the host computer system. Often the same information found online can also be found in already-owned, printed indexes and abstracts. The library staff can decide to make online and CD-ROM services like all other reference services and put the costs into the operating budget (usually by cutting some other part of the budget); or the staff can decide that these "enhanced" services must be paid for in part by the patron. As more and more full-text and graphic information becomes available, such charges are likely to become more common. Prischl and Montgomery (1986, p. 350) see the issues this way:

> Nothing is free, some services are offered as traditional fare while others, such as external online searching, may carry a direct user fee. This question is not only philosophical, but very practical because each service bears an opportunity cost; that is, if you choose to do one thing, you give up something else.

Readers interested in studying this dilemma are referred to the fee-or-free reading list at the end of this chapter.

(4) How will the library reference staff deal with increased demand for document delivery?

When library information services were limited to materials available at the library, or through very slow interlibrary-loan operations, document delivery was not a major problem. Based on the principle of "least effort," most users simply settled for what was immediately available. Online and CD-ROM systems let users know about resources in many locations. At the same time, the delivery systems from remote sites are improving through FAX delivery or through online document-ordering systems. It is no longer a question of "can we get the documents quickly?" Rather, the question is "who will pay for document delivery by FAX or through online ordering systems?"

Some FAX systems use heat-sensitive paper to print the materials sent by telecommunications, which means that another copy must be made if the user wishes to retain that copy for any length of time, thus doubling the user (or library) costs. Installing a FAX card in the workstations makes it possible for the FAX process to be integrated with a workstation, so that documents are downloaded into a disk file as they are received. However, reference staff should take note of potential copyright violations of such activities (what happens to the disk file after the patron gets a copy?) The cost of telephone time and equipment use also needs careful thought.

Document-delivery brokers (large and small) charge for their services. The library can deliver a wide range of documents, but how does the library finance that delivery? Many academic libraries have established a fee-based document-delivery system. A number of research libraries will not respond to any interlibrary-loan transaction without assessing a fee from the requestor.

In libraries where there is an online public-access catalog (as a form of local area network), the library's public has an efficient reference key to the library's collection. Because of the ways in which the library's collection-information database is indexed, it is possible to search this catalog in much more powerful ways than a manual search through the card catalog. Boolian logical operators (*and*, *or*, *not*) and the ability to specify which indexes are to be searched (keyword, author, title, subject) give the public powerful search tools—if the public can use the keyboard and understand the display on the screen. One story currently circulating notes that a user kept pushing the "help" key and ignoring the display on the screen until a library staff member arrived, thinking that was the function of the key (to call for human help). Every online catalog system used by the library's public needs to be easy to use. Even then, training will be necessary.

Other Information Service Functions

Many public services departments provide additional reference and information services by creating local databases or indexes to regional or local publications. A typical example of such a service is indexing a local newspaper. In the past, such indexing was done on three-by-five cards, and was updated as the reference staff could get to it. With the advent of word-processing programs, some libraries began to prepare newspaper indexes by creating a file and updating it on a regular basis: placing entries in their appropriate alphabetical place or using a simple database that could be sorted by entry. More recently, reference departments have been utilizing indexing application software from various vendors to create indexes and keep them up to date. It is also possible to use the indexing function in more expensive word processors to create such indexes. Other bibliographies and lists can be maintained in the same ways. In a local area network system, such files can be available to the library's public from any workstation on the system. Several libraries have moved toward the integration of locally produced indexes, commercial indexes on CD-ROM, and the library online catalog.

In schools and academic libraries, materials are often placed on reserve in order to control access to a limited resource. Finding what is on reserve for what course during what timespan can be very difficult in a manual finding system. Library public-services departments are moving such reserve lists into their online catalog systems, or creating databases available to the library's public at the library or from remote sites.

Conclusion

Use of workstations and local area networks by the library management and staff is not the same thing as their use by the library's public. Ease of use and security of files and equipment are major issues in every public-access situation. The larger and more diverse the library's public is, the more critical both issues become. Sophisticated patrons can compromise the library's system. Different information needs and different levels of computer expertise create problems in the design of a public-access system that will meet all of the public's needs.

The library staff can expect to be involved in instruction on a continuing basis. New publics will demand instruction, and the old publics will want more complex instruction. Application programs, screen displays, and on-screen instructions all need continuing evaluation as the public uses the systems. Once the public has access, they will want better access—or they will go to sources where they can get the access they want.

Further Reading

Fee versus Free

Buckland, M. K. 1988. Library materials: Paper, microform, database. *College & Research Libraries* 49 (March): 117–22.
Curley, A. 1986. *Fees for library service: Current practice and future policy.* New York: Neal-Schuman.

Dougherty, R. M. 1987. Who is really willing to pay? *Journal of Academic Librarianship* 8 (May): 67.

Giacoma, P. 1989. *The fee or free decision: Legal, economic, political, and ethical perspectives for public libraries*. New York: Neal-Schuman.

Kibirige, H. M. 1983. *The information dilemma: A critical analysis of information pricing and the fee controversy*. Westport, Conn.: Greenwood Press.

Turock, B. J. 1987. Fees: A hot potato. *The Bottom Line* 1 (4): 3.

Weinland, J. M., and McClure, C. R. 1987. Economic considerations for fee-based library services: An administrative perspective. *Journal of Academic Librarianship* 8: (Spring): 53–68.

Williams, S. F. 1987. To charge or not to charge: No longer a question? *The Reference Librarian* 19: 125–36.

Public Use of CD-ROMs

Akeroyd, J. 1988. CD-ROM as an online public access catalog. *The Electronic Library* 6 (April): 120–24.

Bills, L. G., and Helgerson, L. W. 1988. CD-ROM public access catalogs: Database creation and maintenance. *Library Hi Tech* 6 (2): 73–115.

Co, F. 1987. CD-ROM and the library: Problems and prospects. *Small Computers in Libraries* 7 (November): 42–48.

Ferguson, D. K. 1987. Electronic information delivery systems: Reports on five projects sponsored by the Fred Meyer Charitable Trust. *Library Hi Tech* 5 (Summer): 65–93.

Micco, H. M., and Smith, I. M. 1989. Designing a workstation for information seekers. *The Reference Librarian* 23: 135–52.

Peters, C. M. 1988. Laser disc-based services for end users. In *End-user searching*. Chicago: American Library Association, 180–96.

Roose, R. J. 1988. Computerized reference tools of the next decade: Taking the plunge with CD-ROM. *Library Journal* 113 (October 15): 56, 61.

Tucker, S. L., et al. 1988. How to manage an extensive laserdisk installation: The Texas A&M experience. *Online* 12 (May): 34–46.

Instructing the Public

Alberico, R. 1987. Media for online instruction. *Small Computers for Libraries* 7 (July): 8–11.

Association of Research Libraries. 1983. *ARL spect kit 93: User instructions for online catalogs in ARL libraries*. Washington, D.C.: ARL (ERIC Document Reproduction Service Number: ED 234 787).

Avery, E. 1985. Teaching online searching: A review of recent research and some recommendations for school media specialists. *School Library Media Quarterly* 13 (Summer): 215–20.

Baker, B. 1986a. A conceptual framework for teaching online catalog use. *Journal of Academic Librarianship* 12 (May): 90–96.

———. 1986b. A new direction for online catalog instruction. *Information Technology and Libraries* 5 (March): 35–41.

Champlin, P. 1985. The online search: Some perils and pitfalls. *RQ* 25 (Winter): 213–17.

Council on Library Resources. 1982. *Training users of online public access catalogs.* Report of a conference sponsored by Trinity University and the Council on Library Resources, January 12–14, 1982 (ERIC Document Reproduction Service Number: ED 235 832).

Dalrymple, P. W. 1984. Closing the gap: The role of the librarian in online searching. *RQ* 24 (Winter): 177–85.

Des Chene, D. 1985. Online searching by end users. *RQ* 25 (Fall): 89–95.

Friend, L. 1986. Identifying and informing the potential end user: Online information seminars. *Online* 10 (January): 47–56.

Hamilton, D. 1985. Library users and online systems: Suggested objectives for library instruction. *RQ* 25 (Winter): 195–97.

Holloway, C. R. 1985. The online catalog: Teaching the user. *RQ* (Winter): 191–94.

Hubbard, A., and Wilson, B. 1986. An integrated management education program . . . Defining a new role for librarians in helping end users. *Online* 10 (March): 15–23.

Kenney, D. K., and Wilson, L. 1985. Education for the online access catalog: A model. *Research Strategies* 3 (Fall): 164–69.

Neilsen, B. 1986. What they say they do and what they do: Instruction through transactional monitoring. *Information Technology and Libraries* 5 (March): 28–34.

———, and Baker, B. 1987. Educating the online catalog user: A model evaluation study. *Library Trends* 35 (Spring): 571–85.

Seiden, P., and Sullivan, P. 1986. Designing a user manual for the online public access catalog. *Library Hi Tech* 4 (Spring): 29–36.

State Library of Pennsylvania. 1987. Online searching: A curriculum guide. *School Library Journal* 33 (May): 59–64.

Software Selection

Dewey, P. R. 1986. *101 software packages to use in your library: Descriptions, evaluations, and practical advice.* Chicago: American Library Association.

Gates, H. 1985. *A directory of library and information retrieval software for microcomputers.* Aldershot, Eng.: Grafton Books.

Intner, S. S. 1988. Developing software collections. In Hannigan, J. A., and Intner, S. S. *The library microcomputer environment.* Phoenix, Ariz.: Oryx Press, 3-21.

Miles, S. G. 1986. *Essential guide to the library IBM PC. Volume 3: Library applications software.* Westport, Conn.: Meckler Publishing.

Watson, R. A., and Taylor, N. 1986. *Directory of microcomputer software for libraries.* Phoenix, Ariz.: Oryx Press.

5

Technical Services Uses

Library workstation: Any workstation configuration, either an especially designed dumb terminal or one based in microcomputer technology, that is: (1) either developed and sold by a library services vendor for use with a particular automated system; or (2) specified as the minimum components required for use of that system and which may be independently assembled from off-the-shelf components. The workstation may or may not be hardwired to a larger computer, chained into a system of terminals, or include a modem.

[Nelson, 1988, p. 12]

The part of library staff most likely to have long-term familiarity with microcomputers, telecommunications, and workstations is the technical-services staff. Many libraries have utilized bibliographic utilities like OCLC, WLN or RLIN through regional networks. Other libraries have utilized "localized" collections of bibliographic information on disk or CD-ROM such as *Bibliofile Catalog Production*. This chapter initially considers the options in telecommunications and local databases from the perspective of the technical-services staff and then looks at particular technical-services functions. Technical-services functions can be divided into two parts: (1) acquisition functions, and (2) cataloging and materials-preparation functions. Both are detailed below.

Remote and Local Options

As business and industry demand high-speed, low-cost telecommunication systems, as well as local access to large databases, library technical-services staff face an increased number of options in finding information about library materials and acquiring and processing those materials into the library system. If a technical-services staff can access current cataloging information at high rates of speed, the costs of finding information on a remote database go down. The following are some of the advantages of telecommunication access: (1) very up-to-date information is available,

(2) charges can be spread across time, and (3) the size of the remote database is larger than any local CD-ROM database available. From the accounting department's standpoint, continuing "open-ended" charges are a problem. How do we know *exactly* what we will spend this year? That depends on how much the system is used. If the library is acquiring a large volume of very up-to-date materials, the technical-services staff needs access to remote databases for cataloging information; or else materials on hand in the library will have to be placed on hold until the next CD-ROM arrives. Libraries updating online catalog databases, will often need high-speed telecommunications capability to locate, modify, and add cataloging information to the database.

In other settings, both acquisitions and cataloging of materials can be based on databases in CD-ROM format, available from vendors and updated on a quarterly basis. These database formats have the advantage of being like a periodical subscription—the library pays for the subscription at the beginning and has unlimited access to the information in the database. Several vendors offer workstations, applications programs, and CD-ROM databases of cataloging information, so that the local library can create catalog copy for local online catalogs or for catalog card production. There is also the option of a CD-ROM system with telecommunications access as needed. Probably the ideal technical-services workstation will provide for both options as integral parts of the workstation. In larger libraries, these workstation-based systems will be expanded into a local area network so that acquisitions, cataloging, and management groups have access to both types of databases on a routine basis. Further reading on CD-ROM and optical-disk applications in libraries will be found at the end of this chapter

Acquisitions

Obtaining materials for the library's public includes finding sources, making orders, tracking orders, and making payment. One major aspect of acquisitions is knowing what the library has on order and what it has received. Workstation and local area network systems should be able to produce information on a particular title (by title, author, publisher, ISBN), or a list of titles on order, by some type of classed array or by particular vendor or publisher. Some systems now allow the library staff to estimate a delivery date and then extract a list of titles not yet on hand but already past estimated delivery date. The staff can then search for the reasons for the delay. In local area network systems, the form-response text for inquiry about titles missing from orders, delayed orders, cancellations, as well as vendors' names and addresses, can be stored as word-processing files and accessed by the staff for inclusion in their communication with vendors and publishers.

Selection of titles can be made much easier by using one of the massive CD-ROM databases now available from Bowker (*Books in Print*) or Baker and Taylor's *BT Link: Database*. Such CD-ROM systems allow for finding exact titles and ordering information, as well as the creation of orders (in print or online formats). Baker and Taylor's system allows for checking on availability in the Baker and Taylor warehouses. *Books in Print* is updated every three months and includes reviews for many items in the database as well as extensive publisher information.

In the acquisitions department, a workstation with a CD-ROM player can become an effective tool for finding titles, publisher information, availability, and producing order forms. In a local area network, the CD-ROM device would be attached to the file server and the information in these databases would also be available to workstations in the library's cataloging, reference, and management groups. Some libraries might consider making this information available to their public if the public can be prevented from creating ordering information, and if the site license allows such access. In fall 1989, Bowker announced a simplified "patron access" module for their *Books in Print CD-ROM*, which offers patrons simplified searching and a special timeout function that returns the patron to the browsing mode if nothing is keyed in after a predetermined wait.

A number of libraries have used database or spreadsheet programs to create and order files. By defining fields appropriately and specifying how those fields should be printed for each record, the library can print pinfeed, multiple-part order forms, or create a purchase order mailing list for a vendor or publisher. If item prices are included, a modified report format can be created to total various accounts or costs by vendors. If such a database or spreadsheet is once created in a library (or library system) it can be accessed by others in the library system by exchanging disks or using a local area network.

Some workstation acquisition systems can be linked into a cataloging system so that catalog records are created at the time of ordering. One example of an integrated technical-services system is Midwest Library Service's *MATTS*, which operates as an acquisition system, including data capture of bibliographic records from remote databases (OCLC, RLIN, WLN) or from the Bibliofile CD-ROM system. Orders for materials can be produced from the bibliographic database or manually typed. The system will either produce printed order forms or transmit orders to vendors via telecommunication systems. Encumbrances, customized fund accounting, special reports, vendor performance, and claiming are all supported. In addition, the system allows for the production of catalog cards, spine labels, and book-pocket labels.

Cataloging at the time of ordering requires careful analysis. What happens to the records of items not delivered? Library acquisitions and technical-services staff will need to analyze their level of "out of print" or "not available" titles before implementing a process of cataloging at order time. Systems should provide the flexibility of creating catalog records (or cards) on receipt of materials. In online catalog systems there is no question that information about what the library has on order, as well as what the library owns, would be useful to staff and to the library's public.

Acquisition functions have large financial factors; the library needs to know what it has encumbered, what has been spent, and what remains. In encumbrances, the library needs to know what companies are owed funds (or vice versa). Several vendors provide foreign-currency exchange programs, which automatically calculate the corrected dollar amounts and can be updated to reflect currency status at any moment. Workstations and local area networks should provide for double entry bookkeeping and detailed breakdown of accounts (into departments, branches, and other divisions). All libraries have to make financial requests and reports to their parent institution in the format required by that institution. Usually libraries also need to make reports for internal purposes, including amounts spent in various subject areas or for specific types of materials. Reports may also be made to network consortia, accrediting agencies, etc. Whatever format one group requires will not be suitable for other groups. Financial spreadsheet programs should allow for reformatting information in whatever format is needed.

The more current accounting information is, the better decisions the acquisition staff can make. Some current integrated systems allow for "real-time" accounting so that order transactions change encumbrance figures, and paying invoices changes budget expenditure figures. Other systems provide such information in a batch mode so that figures of today's work are available the next day. Various spreadsheet functions, allowing for percentages and other formulas, are included.

Unless the library is very large, the acquisition staff is also responsible for the ordering of serial publications. The inflation factor for cost of these publications varies tremendously from one library to another, because no two libraries have the same mix of serial publications. Workstation-based or local-area-networked acquisition systems should allow the staff to build longitudinal cost studies of the serial collection. Some of the integrated systems packages have complex formulas for calculating the weighted costs of serials over time. The ability to study cost trends in this area is critical for ongoing library operations. Because of incredible cost increases in the serial world, the library that does not have a handle on its serial cost trends can end up with the entire acquisition budget committed to a serials collection.

Cost-trend analysis does not replace difficult management decisions about what serial subscriptions to cancel, but it does identify high-cost serials, which are candidates for reconsideration based on the library's goals and the use of the particular serial title. In a local area network, such serial-cost-control information should be available on demand from the library management workstations. In non-network situations, the format of the serial cost data should be compatible with the spreadsheet programs used by library management.

If serial check-in and claiming is a part of the acquisition staff's responsibility, the staff will want to collect data, not only about serials, but also about vendors. Discounts, delivery fulfillment, claims handling (did they get it for us and how long did it take?), and time lag on cancellations are useful information for library decision making.

In libraries that have a local area network available to the public in the form of an online catalog, the technical-services staff may face the large task of converting serial records so that they will become part of the online catalog database. Some libraries have followed the practice of cataloging serials using the same system through which they catalog monographs. These libraries will have minimum difficulty in integrating their serials holdings into the online catalog system. Other libraries have used totally separate systems for serials and other titles and will face a massive conversion process, if the library's public (and the staff) are to have access through the online catalog. Conversions have been accomplished in-house by recataloging or through a vendor to convert records to a standard and format acceptable in the library's online catalog system.

Cataloging and Materials Preparation

The technical-services staff and library management are concerned with the processing of what we have on hand, how long it is taking to move materials into public use, and detailed catalog-record information on particular titles. Since library networking tends to demand that MARC-type formats be utilized, the technical-services staff of many libraries has worked with terminals and workstations for many years in order to access MARC-type records. Many online catalog and circulation systems have been created in non-MARC formats; but the library that contemplates sharing resources with other libraries will need to plan for MARC-like records, which can be shared across several types of systems. The cataloger's workstation (Curtis, 1988, p. 46) was developed because of the library interest in having character sets (including diacritic marks), which can truly reflect the information found in printed resources. Most major computer manufacturers could not respond to this need because libraries were not a large enough market. OCLC began to develop OCLC terminals which provided the necessary character set. Later RLN utilized the IBM color-graphics adapter to generate diacritic marks. As new machine capabilities emerged, the bibliographic-utility vendors began to utilize standard microcomputer hardware capabilities to provide library technical-services options.

OCLC introduced the M300 workstation in 1984. The IBM PC machine was enhanced with a chip containing the OCLC/ALA character set, controlled by the OCLC terminal software, which allowed use of the original IBM character set or the OCLC/ALA set. OCLC also added its own input/output board and an interface panel with additional serial ports. The keyboard was modified to include color-coded keys, with OCLC function keys permanently labeled. Options that have been added include: enhanced memory, hard-disk drives, a CD-ROM unit, and a modem. After IBM introduced the IBM PC XT model, OCLC began delivery on a modified XT called the M300xt. Nelson (1988) gives a detailed description of the M300 and M300xt workstations, as well as their successor, the M310.

In 1987 to 1988, OCLC moved to the WYSEpc 286 (Model 2112), as IBM discontinued the whole PC line for the PS/2 series. This workstation system was designated the M310. This system has a much faster speed and a high-capacity 5¼-inch disk drive. A later addition uses the faster 80386 chip. The WYSE systems do not utilize the typical IBM and clone architecture of a mother board onto which other boards are mounted. Instead, The CPU and memory are on a CPU card which is mounted on a backplane. Upgrading of the system is simplified by the fact that one CPU and memory system can be removed and another installed. Because of this design, the OCLC M310 has only two slots available for local use, since OCLC uses five for its particular applications.

Almost all vendors of cataloging workstations are moving to adapt the technology of faster machines, better graphic displays, and access to CD-ROM players. Library Corporation's Bibliophile is a self-contained workstation with high-resolution graphics, sound, and a silent printer. The workstation can be enhanced to include eight workstations. For the library's public, the workstation provides sound output (prerecorded), Boolean searching, profiling of user tastes, and a bulletin board with message function.

CLSI markets their workstation based on WYSE equipment including the Cataloger's Workstation, which allows for the maintenance of MARC records using the ALA character set. In addition, records can be downloaded from OCLC Micro Enhancer disks, or from remote databases (OCLC, RLIN, Utlas). Geac Corporation also uses WYSE equipment in their Professional Services Terminal as a part of their Library Information

System. High-resolution graphics and connection of workstations is provided through a special daisychain interface card.

Because of enhancing workstation designs and new software and services, OCLC produced a *Communication and Access Planning Guide* (1987) to assist librarians in determining specific service and appropriate access methods for utilizing the OCLC services. The *Planning Guide Supplement* (1987) provides several case studies of library service assessment and a description of the varied OCLC online, retrospective conversion, resource sharing, reference, and local systems options. Even if a library is not contemplating OCLC services, a careful study of these two documents is helpful in determining types and capacities of cataloging workstations.

Vendors can now offer online catalogs in CD-ROM format with regular vendor updating, produced from information sent by the library's cataloging workstation (or sent in on floppy disks). CD-ROM catalogs are typically bibliographic records in MARC format that come with applications programs so that the CD-ROM database can be searched by library staff or the public.

General Research Corporation's *LaserGuide* provides the public with a basic search and a "power" search. Basic search provides author, title, and subject access to a specified index. Power search provides the use of a Boolian AND and OR through placing words in appropriate boxes on the screen. Auto-Graphics Corporation offers *Impact* CD-ROM catalogs, which allow the staff to select the order and number of bibliographic elements that appear on the screen as well as detailed holding information. Public-access options are displayed on the screen, indicating which of the various IBM-type function keys to push for what function.

Brodart offers the *LePac* CD-ROM catalog with a browse function as well as a "fill-in-the-blanks" form for searching in combinations of bibliographic record fields. Library Corporation's *Intelligent Catalog* provides more varied functions and is more complex in use. Libraries using this system must use Library Corporation's equipment, which includes an internal CD-ROM drive, removable hard disk, thermal printer, and lockable workstation desk. This CD-ROM system allows for browsing of the library's collection from a "found" call number in either direction. The system also offers a number of modifications that can be made by the staff including display format and search scope.

The currently available equipment allows for a variety of special services. For example, the OCLC *CJK350 System* provides three software packages for online cataloging, card production, and word processing of records containing Chinese, Japanese, or Korean vernacular characters. *Interlibrary Loan Micro Enhancer* package provides software for use with the interlibrary loan subsystem.

An additional OCLC service, *MICROCON*, provides a way for libraries to enter search keys on a diskette, which is then sent to OCLC for matching with records in the online catalog.

Other vendors (Bibliofile, etc.) make use of large databases stored on CD-ROM devices as a source of cataloging information. Workstations with CD-ROM devices are used with special applications programs to search for bibliographic records, modify them to local library usage, and create a cataloging database. This database may or may not be part of an online catalog system.

At a still simpler level, several vendors provide application software for creating catalog records and either catalog cards or a catalog database that can be used as the basis of an online catalog system. Several of the circulation system vendors (Follett, Winnebago) provide a conversion service in which the library can supply Library of Congress numbers or ISBN data and the vendor will provide catalog records in a MARC format for use with the vendor's online catalog system. Conversion of MARC records is also supported. As online circulation systems store more bibliographic-record information, and online catalog systems include a circulation inventory control module, the library staff will need to study their requirements very carefully. A full-blown integrated system provides a wonderful array of services: acquisitions, catalog record creation, public-access database, varieties of library management information, interlibrary loan, and access to remote databases. Not every library needs all of these functions integrated into one local area network.

It may be that the library really needs to gain inventory control of its collection and patrons. Then online, bar-code-based circulation systems are appropriate. Before converting an entire library's holdings into a MARC-type database, the library staff needs to ask, "who uses our catalog now, and what are they looking for?" A library's public may want access to specific titles, authors, or formats, or to very broad subject categories. If that is the case, many currently available bar-code-based circulation systems will provide all of the access that the public needs: title searches, author searches, format types, a limited set of subject categories. The online public access catalog for such a library may simply be a multiunit local area network that supports an online circulation system, allowing the public to browse the title, author, format, and subject category fields, and (perhaps) to place reserves or do their own check-out of materials.

Circulation Systems

Control of library materials with a circulation system (manual or automated) is an inventory-control problem. The library staff and users need to know not only what the library owns (from the catalog), but also where specific items are at the moment. The retail industry has been utilizing bar codes (product marking codes) for a number of years to control inventory in the retail business. More recently they have developed a one-way circulation system familiar to everyone at the grocery check-out line. This system records items as they are sold and can be used to create weekly, monthly, or seasonal purchase orders for replacements. Another major use of such systems is "weeding" of inventory items that do not sell, or sell at a rate which indicates lack of consumer interest.

Much the same type of inventory control can be created in workstation-based circulation systems (as part of integrated systems or as stand-alone operations). The relationship between the vendor of a workstation-based circulation system and library staff is very important. Many library staff members will be utilizing computers for the first time during this process. An incredible number of things can either go wrong or not function as described in the documentation. Changes in the hardware available, updates to software, and "fixes" to system problems can cause the library staff to confront a system that is not functioning as it did at the vendor's demonstration. Selection of a vendor who will support the library through the installation and testing of the system is critical.

Vendors of such circulation systems are listed in Figure 5.

Libraries considering workstation-based circulation systems for the first time—even if they are not considering a fully integrated library automation program—will need to carry out several important steps before automating circulation. Traditionally considered to be technical-service preparation tasks, these tasks are now often done by the public-services staff because of the collection-management aspects of the process. These steps include carefully weeding the materials collection, preparing materials for the system, preparing a circulation database and a patron database, testing the system in actual work situations, and making a decision about patron access to the system.

Weeding

No matter what the size of the library collection, no library can afford to pay the costs of preparing junk for automated circulation. In many libraries, the process of implementing automated circulation allows the staff to reevaluate the collection, discarding materials that are in poor condition, show little evidence of use, or are outdated. Since every item in the collection must be handled during the preparation process, implementing careful evaluation procedures for weeding can be beneficial—not only because of cost savings (for staff and bar codes)—but also because of the improved quality of the remaining collection and the knowledge gained of areas of the collection in need of new materials. For the library's public, a good

Figure 5.
Sample Suppliers of Circulation Systems

Vendor	Hardware	Prices
CASPR 10311 S. De Anza Cupertino, CA 95014 408-446-3075	Macintosh	Mac Library System $1,695 single-user $4,995 mutliuser with $195 per terminal MacCards $169
Charles Clark Co. 170 Keyland Court Bohemia, NY 11716 800-247-7009	IBM	Molli Circ/Catalog $1,500 Circulation only $750
Columbia Computing Services 8101 E. Prentice Ave. Englwood, CO 80111 800-663-0544	IBM	Circulation $1,095 Catalog $1,325 Acquisitions $1,325 Serials, $545 MARC Interface $545
COMpanion Consulting 10101 Bubb Rd. Cupertino, CA 95014 408-446-9779	Macintosh	Mac BOOK to Mac Book II Plus $995–$5,995 depending on modules
Data Trek, Inc. 167 Saxony Rd. Encinitas, CA 92024 800-876-5484	IBM	Datalog circulation, catalog, acquisitions, serials, $995 each. $2,495 for three modules
Follett Library Software 4506 NW Highway Crystal Lake, IL 60014 800-323-3397	IBM	Circ Plus $995 Catalog Plus $1,295 Textbook Plus $1,695
Library Automation Products 875 Avenue of the Americas New York, NY 10001 212-967-7440	IBM	The Assistant $6,270 Modules: single-user $1,800, multiuser $2,500
Library Corp., Inc. One Research Park Inwood, WV 25428 800-624-0559	Proprietary hardware and software for catalog. IBM other functions	Bibliofile Intelligent Catalog $2,770. Circulation $3,500 one-time maintenance $975
Media Flex, Inc. P. O. Box #1107 Champlain, NY 12919 518-298-2970	IBM	Mandarin circulation and catalog $2,500. Multiuser $3,000 per site

Utlas Corp. 80 Bloor St., W. Toronto, Ontario Canada M5S 2V1 416-923-0890	IBM	MSeries 10 Licenses: Circulation $3,375 Catalog $2,700 for multiusers. Also setup and maintenance costs
Winnebago Software 121 S. Marshall Caledonia, MN 55921 507-724-5411	IBM	Circulation, Catalog $995. Combined $1,695

collection without a lot of garbage is preferable to one with lots of materials—often materials that are outdated, in poor condition, or inaccurate. The rule remains: "weed first, bar code second."

Preparation of Library Materials

Library materials can be ordered from vendors with bar codes attached and with information for several microcomputer-based circulation systems on an enclosed floppy disk. However, the bulk of the library collection is not bar coded; and, therefore it must be removed from the shelf and bar coded, the bar code number recorded on the shelflist, and a protective cover placed over the bar code. Library staff may choose to bar code materials as they are used or attempt to bar code the bulk of the collection before building the materials database. Either way, the process is labor intensive. Some libraries will place the bar code in a protected inside cover area; others will use the back or front of the book. Because of varieties in book width and nonprint formats, the spine of the materials is rarely used.

Creation of a Circulation Database

Basic information on each item in the collection must be entered into a workstation-based database on a hard disk. The vendor's software usually provides a menu-driven program for such data entry. Such a database is often *not* a full bibliographic record or a full MARC record, but rather, minimal information to provide for circulation control—often including author, short title, call numbers, Library of Congress number or ISBN, cost, and information about major subject categories of the item. Such database creation is expensive, and vendors provide data-entry services on a per-item cost, either by typing the shelflist of the library or by retrieving data from a larger database owned by the vendor. The ISBN or Library of Congress number is included so that the library may later use that identifying number with a vendor to create MARC-like records for public-access online catalog systems. Again, library staff may create the database "on the run" as materials are used (or returned), or they may create the database before operating the system.

Creation of a Patron Database

A patron database is essential to the control of materials. The library and its patrons need to know what is in circulation, and the library staff needs to know who has what materials. In systems where overdue fines are used, such patron information must include patron addresses and often telephone numbers. Many libraries have several categories of patrons: faculty, students, special, interlibrary loan. Most workstation-based circulation systems control patrons in the same way materials are controlled: by using a bar code for each patron. In some settings, patron bar code information is kept in a file at the circulation desk; in other situations, patrons are issued embossed cards with bar code information on the card.

Testing the System

One cannot assume that when the databases are created, the system will run without error. A wide variety of bar code printing exists, light pen devices vary in their ease of use, and the combination of software, hardware, and firmware cards may require adjustments. Library staff will need to allow for a test-run period, during which any difficulties in reading bar codes; accessing the databases; and failures of printers, displays, or other software functions should be carefully documented and cleared up with the vendor. Obviously, the library will need to run the manual circulation system in tandem with the online system until the bugs are worked out. Unfortunately, this fact has not always been obvious to library managers, and libraries have ended up with no circulation files at all.

Public Access

The control of the library's inventory at the circulation desk is expensive because of staffing that location. A number of libraries have turned to "self check-out" systems in which the library's public does their own check-out of materials, either on-site or from remote terminals. This particular form of public access to workstations has a number of problems: (1) the need to train the public in the use of the system, (2) the potential for abuse of equipment and software, and (3) the possibility of patron manipulation of circulation data, compromising the security of the system.

Beyond Cataloging

Most library technical-services departments are also responsible for making materials ready for public use. That process includes marking ownership on the materials, placing book pockets and cards (or bar codes) in the book, and spine labelling. A number of computer-based cataloging systems allow the creation of spine labels, book pockets, and book cards, as well as bar codes, during the catalog-record-creation process. Typically, specific fields of information from the catalog record are saved and routed to a printer set up with pinfeed labels and cards and pockets. The cataloging workstation operator edits the catalog record and then issues the command to have labels, etc., printed. Sometimes this information is stored in a separate file so that it can be called up by another book-preparation workstation and the materials printed at that time.

Retrospective Conversion

Another major concern of library technical-services departments is retrospective conversion. More and more libraries are moving toward some form of online catalog database. These libraries face the gigantic task of converting their major finding tool, the catalog, into a local database. Some libraries will already have two other databases: (1) a circulation system with brief author, title, and call number information for every copy of every title in the system, and (2) a remote database, built with a vendor, and used for the production of catalog cards (often OCLC). Technical-services staff and library management face a number of decisions: (1) how much of the collection is to be converted, (2) who will do the conversion, (3) what standards to follow, and (4) how localized the database is to become.

Facing a large manual system, the library staff often decides that not everything needs to be converted at once. The library management will need to decide what the priority areas are: circulating collection? reference? reserves? special collections? nonprint? Staff will need information on collection use to make intelligent decisions about priorities. In libraries where local area network circulation systems have been operating, such statistical data will have been collected over a period of time. Other libraries will use publication date of materials as a criterion for inclusion in the conversion process: if it was published after a specific date, we convert it. In smaller libraries, the conversion process may be done "on the fly" by converting materials as they circulate and converting all materials acquired after a certain date. Often a special conversion workstation is setup to deal with materials as they come back from circulation or as they arrive from the acquisitions department.

Library management has a number of options in deciding who will convert the bibliographic records. The conversion may be done as a total in-house operation, using the library staff, or by hiring additional temporary help. If additional staff are hired, there will be additional costs and delays because that staff will require training in the use of the conversion programs, in local library rules, and in procedures for catalog entry. Alternatively, the management may decide that all conversion is going to be done by a vendor to locally defined standards. Here the decision is between paying staff costs and paying a vendor. Using library staff to convert bibliographic records will mean that the staff cannot continue to do all of their regular work. Backlogs in acquisitions and cataloging can result. Vendor-produced databases are the quickest and probably the cheapest way to do a conversion project.

The quality of vendor conversion will depend almost entirely on the communication between technical-services staff and the vendor about what records are now available and what the file bibliographic record is to contain. The staff will need to draw a sample of records, have a trial conversion, and see if the records produced meet local needs. In any such conversion there will be "exception" records which require local editing. If the card catalog has a long history, the technical services staff will need to clarify issues related to tracings, call number formats, notes, what fields of local information are to be used, etc. The monitoring of quality of bibliographic records produced will continue throughout the project. If the technical-services staff is operating in a workstation environment, someone may be assigned the tasks of pulling up converted records and monitoring particular MARC II fields. The editing of "exception" records, which could be fully converted by the vendor, can be handled in this same way. In a local area network environment, the database of converted records, exception records, and rules would be available at a number of workstations.

Conclusion

Workstations have a long history in library technical services. As libraries develop local area networks, the technical-services system will need to be integrated into the management and public-access systems of the library. For larger libraries, integrated systems are available that will provide multiple-function workstations, linked through a local area network, for all these services. Many library management groups will want to integrate these systems one at a time so that each one can be tested operationally before full integration. In the future, such integrated systems, built on modules, will be accessible to smaller libraries as the costs of such modules (and related equipment) continues to decline.

Further Reading

Anderson, C. 1989. Using technology [Books in Print Plus]. *Wilson Library Bulletin* 63 (June): 92–93.

Bloechle, M. K. 1987. Steamlining book ordering through the use of BIP + in the CD-ROM medium. *Texas Library Journal* 63 (Summer): 56–57.

Brunnell, D. H. 1988. Comparing CD-ROM products. *CD-ROM Librarian* 3 (March): 14–18.

Chen, Ching-chih. 1989. *HyperSource on optical technologies*. Chicago: Library and Information Technology Association, American Library Association.

———. 1989. Survey on the use of optical products in libraries and information centers. *Microcomputers for Information Management* 6 (March): 73–74.

Demas, S. G. 1987. Comparing BIP bibliographies on CD-ROM: An expert evaluates two trade booklists on compact disc (Anybook and BIP +). *American Libraries* 18 (May): 332–35.

Desmarais, N. 1988. An evaluation of the PC-laser library from the Library Corporation. *Optical Information Systems* 8 (January–February): 14–18.

———. 1989. The serials directory/EBSCO CD-ROM. *CD-ROM Librarian* 4 (April): 28–33.

Eaton, N. L., and Schwerin, J. B. 1986. CD-ROM optical disc technology in libraries: Acceptance and implementation. In *Proceedings of the Association of College and Research Libraries, Fourth National Conference, Baltimore, Md.* Chicago: Association of College and Research Libraries, American Library Association.

Ferraro, A. J. 1988. Ulrich's PLUS: A high-performance, low-cost alternative to online serials reference systems. *Serials Librarian* 14 (3–4): 121–23.

Ferrell, M. S., and Parkhurst, C. A. 1987. Using LaserQuest for retrospective conversion of MARC records. *Optical Information Systems* 7 (November–December): 396–400.

Fink, T. 1988. LaserCat goes to high school. *Wilson Library Bulletin* 62 (March): 55–56.

Giesbrecht, W. W. 1988. Comparison of three CD-ROM cataloguing tools: Bibliofile, LaserCat, LaserQuest. *School Libraries in Canada* 9 (Fall) 23–27.

Holloway, C. 1987. Books in Print and Ulrich's on CD-ROM: A preliminary review. *Online* 11 (September): 57–61.

Lowell, G. The Library of Congress on CD-ROM. In *CD-ROM: The new papyrus*. Ed. S. Lambert and S. Ropiequet. Redmond, Wash.: Microsoft Press, 517–26.

Online Computer Library Corporation. 1987. OCLC compact disk study. *Laserdisk Professional* 1 (May): 44–49.

Saffady, W. 1988. Optical storage products at the 1988 AIIM Conference. *Optical Information Systems* 8 (September–October): 232–41.

Urbanski, V. 1988. Resources and technical service news: Ring out the old, ring in the new (announcements of new software packages and CD-ROM products). *Library Resources and Technical Services* 32 (October): 409–13.

Watson, P. D. 1987. CD-ROM catalog—Evaluating LePac and looking ahead. *Online* 11 (September): 74–80.

6

Ergonomics and Library Operations

Once the decision has been made to purchase a particular system and the conversion of bibliographic data has been completed, however, most libraries proceed to introduce their users to the system simply by placing terminals in major service areas. The planning and thought that go into the initial process of choosing a particular system seldom go into the purchase of public terminal equipment.

[Kenney and Wilson, 1988, p. 46]

If the library staff and the public are going to have workstations, and those workstations are going to be connected to one another so that efficient communication and effective teamwork can be done, careful human-factors planning of equipment and the work environment is required. Such human factors include sensory, physical, intellectual, and motivational aspects that can influence the design and placement of equipment in the workplace.

Personal Computers and Typewriters

Personal computers with video display terminals (VDTs) are not the same as previous typewriter workstations. Miller (1983, 1986) has pointed out these differences:

VDT displays are more reflective than paper, creating glare that may be annoying and uncomfortable.
VDTs emit light, whereas paper reflects it.
VDTs are vertically positioned whereas most paper is read horizontally.
VDTs may not display symbols with the same quality as some paper documents.

VDT devices usually have a cathode ray tube for display of information. Some display devices may use light emitting diodes or liquid-crystal displays. If the display is a cathode ray tube, the information is displayed by playing a beam of light across the inner face of the tube, which is coated with phosophor. The beam of light constantly refreshes the dots of light on the screen so that the image remains.

Ergonomic factors related to cathode ray VDT devices will depend on the use of the device. Demanding visual tasks that are going to be done over extended periods of time require the best-quality images. The American Society of Safety Engineers (1985, p. iv-3) has divided tasks associated with VDT devices as follows:

> legibility tasks are those tasks requiring accurate perception of individual digits or letters.
>
> readability tasks require the determination of the meaning of groups of digits or letters.

Visual tasks involving familiar materials are readability tasks, and the sharpness of individual characters is not as critical because the operator's cognitive processes can fill in the voids. Visual or typing tasks involving symbols in nonsense sequence or grouping unfamiliar symbols into formulas or words are legibility tasks because the operator does not have previous experience with the particular text.

Images on VDT devices also affect the ease of use. CRT devices can display images as dark characters on bright backgrounds (negative contrast) or as light characters on a dark background (positive contrast). Most VDT devices use this latter method for initial display; although programming can alter the display.

Other factors which affect the display include contrast, color, flicker, and character size and shape. Contrast is defined as the ratio between the brightness (luminance) of one object and another. The human eye must have contrast to perceive images. It is hard to read light text on light paper or dark text on dark paper. In VDT devices, the background brightness is crucial. Since there are large differences in individual preferences for contrast, VDT devices should allow adjustment of the background contrast by the user. Many VDT devices allow the adjustment of background and character (foreground) brightness. Poorly designed VDT devices may vary the brightness of characters or background in different sections of the screen.

Color of foreground and background is largely a matter of individual preference. People who have a particular screen or character combination tend to prefer it. In some cases of color blindness or limitation, specific color combinations may make the VDT device usable by individuals. For example, a word-processing package may allow the user to select not only the background and foreground color for display, but also the ways in which bold and underlined test will appear.

Flicker on VDT devices is caused by the fact that when a beam of electrons "excites" a place on the CRT, it glows; but as soon as that beam leaves a spot, the spot begins to fade. If an image is to remain on the screen, it must be constantly refreshed. When this "refreshing" does not occur frequently enough, the display appears to blink (fade, bright, fade, bright) or flicker. If the image of the screen is very bright, flicker is more apparent. If the office area around a VDT screen is dark, the images on the screen will appear to flicker more. If the display shows dark characters on a light background, there will be more flicker because of the large lighted areas on the screen. Flicker is more noticeable in areas of the screen outside of the direct line of sight. These peripheral areas seem to stop flickering when the user looks directly at them. The ways in which people perceive (or do not perceive) flicker varies greatly. As people get older, they tend to notice flicker less. Flicker can be controlled by increasing the refresh rate on the screen or by a higher-quality screen coating that holds its luminescence longer.

Character size and shape on VDT devices is determined by a pattern of dots in what is called a "dot matrix." Small dot matrices are five by seven dots (five dots wide, seven dots high) and do not allow for clear distinction between text characters. Larger dot matrices allow great distinction between different characters and symbols. Larger matrices allow for larger characters to be created, or for better detail in individual characters. Larger matrices also allow for lower-case letters with descenders—the parts of a letter that extend below the line, as when *y* or *p* is written. The larger the matrix, the more-detailed resolution each character may have. Characters built with square dots rather than circular dots will fill in more space between dots and create an easier-to-read character. Figure 6 illustrates these dot-matrix character differences.

Figure 6.
Dot Matrix Character

Nine by seven matrix with true descender

The height of characters determines the distance from which they can be viewed. As a viewer moves further away from an object (like a letter on the screen), it appears to grow smaller. The recommended angle for viewing characters is described by the angle created when viewing the top and bottom of the character. This angle is measured in minutes of arc. Ten to twelve minutes of arc are recommended for readability; fourteen to sixteen minutes of arc are recommended for legibility. When viewed from 13 inches away, a character should be .04 inches high. Double the distance requires a character which is .08 high. The resolution (sharpness, crispness, or blurriness) of the dots that make up characters, will affect both legibility and readability. The precision of focus of the electron beam on the VDT's phosphor determines resolution. Resolution of dots on all areas of the screen should be constant. Figure 7 illustrates the effect of viewing distance on character size requirements.

Glare can be a major problem with VDT devices. Reflected glare is the glare that bounces off objects—the face of the VDT. Direct glare is the glare received from a source of light such as a light bulb. Since VDT screens are a source of light, they have the potential of giving off both kinds of glare. Manufacturers of VDT devices may use etched glass or a film coating to reduce glare factors. Other means of reducing glare include circular polarized shields, neutral density shields, micromeshes (a weave of dark synthetic threads), or hoods that block reflected light from the VDT screen. All of these devices are available from computer suppliers. (American Society of Safety Engineers, 1985, iv-8-10) The *perfect* VDT device is probably too expensive to design and manufacture because VDTs are put to so many

---

Figure 7.
Angle of Viewing

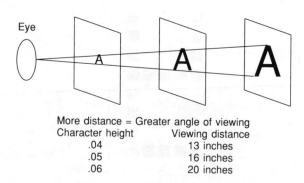

More distance = Greater angle of viewing

Character height	Viewing distance
.04	13 inches
.05	16 inches
.06	20 inches

different uses. Knowing how the device will be used, and for what periods of time, will assist the library administration in the selection of appropriate VDT monitors.

Any consideration of the lighting problems related to VDT displays must take into account the total illumination of the office area. Usually 550 to 700 lux of illumination in the surrounding area is satisfactory. Windows are especially important since they let in natural light. Some means of controlling that light must be provided by blinds, curtains, or reflective film. Natural light from windows should not be *behind* the VDT. Interior lighting with electric lamps can be used to control the amount of light at various places in an office. The use of rheostats and different intensity bulbs can be used to fine-tune the amount of light. Overhead fluorescent lights mounted on untextured ceilings create a large amount of glare. Sometimes task lamps, which illuminate a particular area (the sheet of paper that is being read), are more useful.

Determining the sources and intensities of light in an office area can assist the library manager in locating workstations so that direct and reflected glare are reduced and the light in various parts of the room is controlled. Since every piece of office equipment can reflect light, care should be taken to have files, desks, fixtures, and other furniture in suitable colors. Often the installation of a textured partition will not only shade a workstation area, but will also reduce the amount of noise transmitted from one area to another. Direct sunlight in front of the workstation should be avoided. The purchaser of a workstation should look for the capacity of the VDT to be tilted and turned from side to side. Since not all individuals using the machine will want the VDT in the same position, ease of movement is important.

Working with Workstations: Human Positions

Grandjean, Hunting, Maeda, and Laubli (1983) point out that people engage in a number of constraining (or static) postures during their workday. They list the following examples:

bending the trunk of the body forward or sideways causes a heavy static load on the muscles of the back

holding arms extended forward in a static effort

keeping an arm and hand outstretched in order to operate a machine may cause muscle fatigue in the shoulder

standing in one place is bad for blood circulation and may cause venous congestions (when we walk, the legs act as pumps: a favorable circulatory situation) the inclination of the head is a postural problem. The recommended angle (from horizontal) for viewing displays when standing is 15 degrees to 45 degrees, and 26 degrees to 50 degrees when sitting.

Possible medical problems associated with bad posture are listed in Figure 8.
The introduction of workstations into the library work environment creates very specific problems. The space in which an individual can work is restricted. Many of the movements of the hands, arms, and head are repeated endlessly. Holding the head in tilted positions due to the placement of the monitor can cause painful neck conditions. Hunting (1980a, 1980b) has systematically studied a number of workplaces equipped with personal computers or terminals including banks, post offices, and typing pools. He found that forward bending of the head causes stiffness in the neck and is increased as the degree of bending increases. Also tiredness, pains, and cramps in the hand increase as lateral motion of the hand increases. Terminal operators reported pain in the areas of the neck, shoulders, arms, and hands, with data entry workers showing the highest incidence of neck, shoulder, arm, and hand difficulties. Many fewer problems were found among typists and "traditional" office workers.
Specific human-factors design principles have been recommended for personal-computer workstation arrangements:

Figure 8.
Medical Problems Associated with Bad Posture

Postures	Risk of Pain or Disease
Standing in one place	Foot and leg problems, varicose veins
Sitting erect without back support	Extensor muscle of the back
Seat too high	Knee or back problems
Seat too low	Shoulder, upper arm problems
Trunk curved forward when sitting or standing	Lumbar region, disk problems
Head inclined forward	Neck and disk deterioration

(1) All workplace dimensions should be suited to the body size of the operator

Since individuals come in a variety of sizes, most workstation tables, keyboard locations, and monitor locations should be adjustable. Tools used with the workstations: copy stands, mouse devices, switches, printer controls, etc., should be arranged so that the worker does not have to strain in any way to reach all of the controls for the system.

Separate means of adjusting desk height and level, positions of source documents, and height and angle of the monitor ensure that appropriate modifications can be mode for each worker. Movable keyboards provide greater flexibility of arrangement. Even the keyboard arrangement (where keys beyond the traditional typewriter keys are placed in the keyboard layout) can be helpful.

(2) Specific areas of concern with workstations will be:

(a) the ability to have comfortable head positions. Placement of monitor and placement of source documents are the greatest influences on head position.

(b) adequate height in the work area (no sense of being boxed in)

(c) adequate horizontal and vertical space for grasping and moving various controls. (Not reaching around, over or behind something or having to move something to another place to use a control.)

(d) adequate space for legs. Tables with aprons, crossbars as leg supports, or machines placed on cabinets with no leg space should be avoided. High-backed chairs that are adjustable for back position and leg room are recommended.

(e) adequate opportunity to rest hands and forearms, while waiting at the keyboard, is necessary. For example, when the keyboard is placed in a keyboard tray that pulls out from under the computer or table, there is often space to rest the hands below the keyboard. Almost everyone who attaches such a device to their workstation comes to use this resting area automatically when they are not actively typing.

(f) keyboard tables or stands should be adjustable so that the operator's arms can form at least a ninety degree angle between the upper arm and the forearm when typing

Figure 9 illustrates these principles.

Some of these factors will not be as important for the occasional user of the system, but care should be taken here; remember how poorly libraries did with the design of card-catalog cabinets, trays, and areas on which to use the card catalog. Card catalogs were designed to store cards efficiently, not to be used by human beings who wished to read information in the catalog and take notes.

Figure 9.
Correct Positioning of Workstation

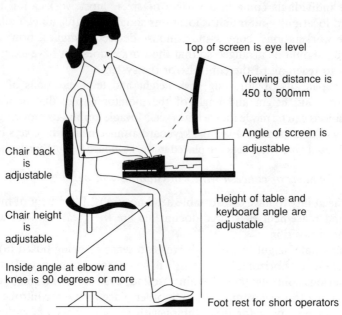

Top of screen is eye level

Viewing distance is
450 to 500mm

Angle of screen is
adjustable

Chair back
is
adjustable

Height of table and
keyboard angle are
adjustable

Chair height
is
adjustable

Inside angle at elbow and
knee is 90 degrees or more

Foot rest for short operators

Keyboard Design

Keyboards are the most commonly used data-entry and response devices in offices. There is wide variation in keyboard design. Several factors are important in selection of keyboards:

detachability—is the keyboard attached to the computer by a long enough cord to allow for a variety of positions for use? People have very individual tastes in how they use the keyboard. Keyboards that are an integral part of the computer housing are harder to steal, but also harder to use.

thickness—keyboards should be 1½ to 2 inches thick if they are to be used on a typical 29-inch-high table. Keyboard design should allow for a "wrist rest" below the lowest range of keys so that a person can rest their arms when not typing.

non-skid bases—the bottom of the keyboard should be non-skid so that the keyboard will not slide out of control on smooth or sloping surfaces.

slope—the angle of slope will depend on the work done and personal preference. Adjustable slope between zero degrees and fifteen degrees is preferred.

profile—seen from the side, keyboards are stepped, sloped, or dished, so that all keys are not at the same level. The idea of sloped keyboards is inherited from typewriter-like devices. Most individuals will be more comfortable with some sloping of the keyboard, especially those who touch-type.

key placement and spacing—keys should be large enough to feel individually and to allow for a legible character to be printed on each key. Does anyone remember the original Commodore Pet keyboard? (very small, keys close together) The operator's fingers should be able to hit one key at a time without accidentally hitting several keys.

keyboard touch—another matter of personal preference. The keyboard should not feel "stiff" or "mushy." Individual experience with other keyboards will influence the reaction to new keyboards. Most microcomputer makers do not provide for adjustment of the keyboard feel.

keyboard feedback—keyboards can be designed to give an audible signal when touched. This feedback is used to inform the user that a key has been depressed. Some keyboards try to imitate the sound of electric typewriter keyboards. Software is available to turn the key click on and off. Where several machines are used in the same area, the quieter the feedback, the better.

keyboard character layout—the two major layouts are QWERTY (named for the keys on the top alphabetical row of the keyboard) and DVORAK (named after its inventor). Few individuals who type have used a DVORAK layout, which was designed to place the most frequently used typewriter keys under the strongest fingers. Prefer QWERTY unless retraining everyone.

keyboard additions—many keyboards now come with number pads, extra function keys, and special control keys mounted on the keyboard base. Sometimes these keyboard additions are placed beside the regular keyboard set; sometimes these keys are placed at the top of the display. Often these additional keys place the typewriter section off-center, usually to the left. If an individual is used to centering his or her chair on the center of the keyboard, adjustment of seat location will be required.

Placement of control keys, back slash key, insert key, delete key vary from model to model. Some software packages allow for modification of keys to different functions, so that the familiar key layout can be replicated on a new keyboard.

keyboard state indicator—some keyboards now come with LED indicators for specific keys, such as the caps lock key, the num lock, and the scroll lock key.

Office Arrangement and Furniture

The placement of a personal-computer workstation is largely determined by the space available and type of tables or desks for placement. Computer supply catalogs are full of examples of types of furniture and accessories that can be purchased to allow for flexible or mobile placement of workstations, VDT devices, and keyboards. Several patterns can be found in the placement of workstations:

(1) Take out the typewriter and put the workstation in its place

First-time personal-computer users often assume that the space and electrical requirements for PCs is the same as typewriters. It is not. Workstations require a means of placing the detached keyboard on a flat surface, a place for the computer itself, several electrical outlets, a place for the VDT device, and a place for the detached printer. Often secretarial workstations have a pair of electrical outlets in the floor or on a column—not enough outlets for all the equipment.

If the VDT device is placed on top of the computer, with the keyboard in front of the computer, a minimum of 30 inches of desk top is required. Often the computer is placed on a small table, which serves as a computer stand and has a drawer where the keyboard unit can be stored when not in use. Some of these stands add a drawer mechanism that allows the keyboard to be suspended in front of the computer when in use, so that a small table can be used. Several of these drawer mechanisms allow for adjustment of height and distance from the front edge of the table, making them useful to a wider range of individuals.

Another option is moving the VDT device to a suspended arm device that can be moved around *above* the table top. If the computer is placed on its side in a vertical computer stand on the floor, the small typewriter-table top can hold the keyboard and the monitor. All of these adjustments assume that the connecting cables will be long enough to reach between devices and that placing the computer in a stand on the floor is safe. Special desks are made to allow for more secure storage of the computer and keyboard.

No matter what is done with the typical typing table or desk extension, another location will need to be found for the printer. Local area networks deal with this problem by placing printers and other output devices in a remote location away from the workstation. The human problem becomes,

"How do I know what I am printing, or that plotting is actually being done without paper jams, or other problems?"

(2) Just put it on the desk

Many managers do not have typing tables or desk extensions (except for that small board that slids out of the right-hand side of the desk, above the top drawer). Often workstations are placed on the desk as a unit: keyboard, computer and monitor. The height of the desk is the problem. Desks are typically two to four inches higher than typing tables. Use of the keyboard is more difficult if the individual must "reach up" to use it. Placement on a side table or mobile unit is to be preferred.

(3) Rebuild the desk environment

Several workstation desk systems are available with special extension surfaces for printers, computers, and keyboards. Sometimes these desk systems allow for the printer and keyboard to be hidden when not in use. Another type of desk system allows for the desk surface to be transparent so that the VDT device can be placed in a sloped tray under that surface and the computer and keyboard can be placed in hidden drawers. Such desk systems allow for viewing the VDT device by looking down (rather than straight ahead), and allow the desk to be used for other purposes when the workstation is not in use. These latter desk systems are expensive (eight hundred to one thousand dollars), and not everyone is comfortable with the viewing arrangement.

Top-of-desk placement of computers has created a demand for small "footprint" machines which take up a minimum of desk space. Careful thought should be given to the "footprint" area of the workstation system being considered. How much tabletop or desk space is required? What is the most comfortable way to use the keyboard and view the screen? Where will the system on/off switches be located? If the workstation requires extensive refitting of the office area, these costs should be taken into account during the planning process.

Wiring

The workstation and local area network planner faces a problem familiar to the early "hi-fi" purchaser. The system comes in components that must be connected with cables. Several of the components require electrical outlets. Often floors are concrete or tile and lack cable conduit. Sometimes offices have suspended ceiling systems, and cables can be run above the office area; but how can they get from the desktop to the ceiling? A variety of wall-mount and power-strip columns are sold to help solve these problems.

Conclusion

Since libraries are moving rapidly to adopt workstations for staff and public, the library staff must be knowledgeable about the impact of workstation design and placement on the people who use them. Managers will want to consult with staff members who are using the workstations to determine the best overall solutions to ergonomic problems. Asking the library's public to test workstation design, location in the library, and screen displays can assist library management in making good choices for public-access workstations and software.

Further Reading

Alden, D. G. 1972. Keyboard design and operation: A review of major issues. *Human Factors* 32: 275–93.

Bergman, T. 1980. *Health protection for operators of VDTs/CRTs.* New York: New York Committee for Occupational Safety and Health.

Brown, B. S.; Dismukes, K.; and Rinalducci, E. J. 1982. Video display terminals and the vision of workers: Summary and overview of a symposium. *Behavior and Information Technology* 1 (April–June): 121–40.

Brown, S. C., and Martins, J. N. T., eds. 1977. *Human aspects of man-made systems.* London: Open University Press.

Byerly, G., and Lindell, S. 1982. Terminals in libraries: Help or hazard? *Library Journal* 107 (November 15): 2146–49.

Cakir, A. 1980. *Visual display terminals: A manual covering ergonomics, workplace design, health and safety, task organization.* New York: Wiley Interscience.

Crawford, W. VDT checklist: 1984. Another look at terminals. *Information Technology and Libraries* 3 (December): 343–53.

Grandjean, E. 1980. *Fitting the task to the man: An ergonomic approach,* 2nd ed. London: Taylor and Francis.

————, and Vigliani, E. 1980. *Ergonomic aspects of visual display terminals.* London: Taylor and Francis.

Kroemer, K. H. E. 1971. Seating in plant and office. *American Industrial Hygiene Association Journal* 32: 633–52.

Kvalseth, T. O. 1982. Design of man-machine systems. In *Handbook of industrial engineering.* Ed. G. Salvendy. New York: Wiley.

————. 1983. *Ergonomics of workstation design.* London: Butterworth.

Library Administration Management Association. 1986. *Training issues in changing technology.* Chicago: LAMA, American Library Association.

Mason, R. 1984. Ergonomics: The human and the machine. *Library Journal* 109 (January 15): 331–32.

National Institute for Occupational Safety and Health. 1981. *Potential health hazards of video display terminals.* Cincinnati, Ohio: The Institute.

Philbin, P. 1982. *CRT's and occupational safety.* Dublin, Ohio: OCLC Library.

Springer, T. J. 1984. Sit on it—Searching for a good chair. *Online* 8 (May): 44–45.

Torok, A. G. 1984. Ergonomics considerations in microcomputing. *Microcomputers for Information Management: An International Journal for Library and Information Services* 1 (September): 229–50.

Wilson, B-R, and Dale, D. 1985. How comfortable is your catalog? *Technicalities* 5 (July): 14–15.

Other Resources

VDT's—Questions and answers. 1984. Washington, D.C.: Computer and Business Equipment Manufacturers Association. Video, 22 minutes, $100. Experts discuss the safety of VDT devices. Consensus is that there is no evidence to suspect devices are unsafe. The importance of proper workplace design and job design to eliminate stress and discomfort are emphasized.

Working with VDT's—The human interfact. 1984. Daly City, Calif.: Krames Communications. Brochure. Gives a brief introduction to human-factors concept in office work using VDT devices. Includes several relaxation exercises and suggestions on rest periods.

Bell Laboratories. 1983. *Video display terminals: Preliminary guidelines for selection, installation and use.* Indianapolis: ATT Technology, Box 46219, Indianapolis, IN 19901. A detailed discussion of ergonomics in design of office furniture, VDT devices, and illumination.

Koffler Group. *Office systems ergonomics report.* Santa Monica, Calif.: The Koffler Group, 3029 Wilshire Blvd., Santa Monica, CA 90403. Monthly newsletter.

7

Protocols, Topologies, Processing, and Procedures

[The general purpose computer system] will be bus-oriented (a wide-band communications line). . . . It will contain multiple computers dedicated to specific functions of the system. The processors will communicate with one another via messages or data blocks in standard form. . . . They will be able to back up one another in the event of failure of any other one. Fault tolerance will be available both at the system level and at the device and component level to accommodate the increased demands of the users for high system availability.

There will no longer be a single, shared storage serving all of the processors. Instead, storage will be dedicated to individual processors or clusters of processors, with the file processor as the central resource.

[Andriole, 1985, p. 116]

This chapter describes workstation and network interconnections, and outlines different types of transmission systems and cabling. Next, it presents mutually agreed-upon procedures and formats for information exchange between computers. These rules and procedures (protocols) have been developed to allow a number of messages to utilize the same channel without conflict. Further reading about published national and international standards are found at the end of the chapter.

Computer-to-Computer Connections

In chapter 1 a simple computer-to-computer connection is discussed. When connections involve two computers, some relatively simple connections can be made. Emmett and Gabel (1986, p. 169) provide a "general solution" RS232 null modem connection, which is shown in Figure 10. They also provide step-by-step illustrations on interconnections between different types and models of microcomputers and software packages.

Figure 10.
Computer-to-Computer Connections

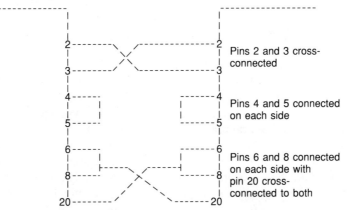

RS232 pin connections between two microcomputers

If a standard design for RS232 connections was carefully followed by every personal computer developer, such connections would be very simple: (1) buy a connecting cable, (2) attach it to the serial ports, (3) mount appropriate communications software in each machine, and (4) run the programs so that one machine sends and the other receives.

Anyone who has tried this operation knows how easily such attempts are foiled. For example, buying cable means knowing what kind of serial outlet (male, female, 25-pin, 9-pin) each computer has. Microsoft corporation's mouse comes with various cables and connectors so that it can be attached to any number of configurations. Manufacturers do not always wire the serial port in the same way. Any attempt to connect two computers via the serial ports should only be done after carefully reading the technical section of the user manual on serial-port configuration. A more recent standard, EIA 449 has a 37-pin connector layout that requires an adapter for use with the RS232 25-pin connector.

Beyond Connecting Two Machines

Why not simply wire all of the computers together using one set of wires for each computer as it is attached to the others? Such connections are called "point-to-point" links. If you have more than two computers to connect, the number of wires rapidly becomes prohibitive, because a wired connection must be maintained between all machines *even when that machine connection is not used.* That is to say, the costs of installation and hardware grow by the square of the number of devices. Once a link is established between two devices, it continues until the connection is broken. Not only is such a scheme expensive when several machines are connected, but the connection is wasted when no information is flowing. If a microcomputer is connected to a laser printer and not using it, the connection is of no value.

To avoid this problem, a network of switching nodes that could create logical links and route messages was developed. The network serves as the link between all of the machines connected to it. A variety of network arrangements are used: STAR, RING, BUS, and TREE.

The STAR network connects each station (node) in a point-to-point link with a common central processor (or file server). For one station to transmit data, it must send a request to the central processor and ask to be connected to another station. Once the central processor has established the circuit link, the two stations can interact directly. The STAR system uses a centralized communications control strategy. Figure 11 shows the STAR network.

Such systems demand a complex central processor which must maintain a number of concurrent data paths. However, the burden on each workstation (node) of the system is minimal.

The RING network contains a set of repeaters joined in a point-to-point link in a closed loop (hence the term *ring*). Information is passed around the loop by the repeater in one direction. The RING network is shown in Figure 12.

Stations are attached to the loop (ring) and data is transmitted in "packets." Packets are bundles of information surrounded by electrical signals which tell the system to which work station the information is going

Figure 11.
STAR Network

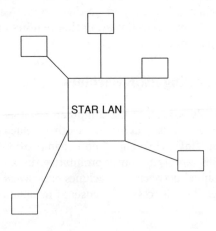

Figure 12.
RING Network

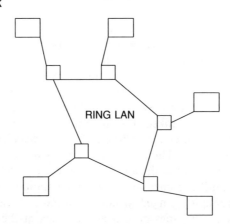

and where the message begins and ends. These signals act in the same way the "beginning of file" and "end of file" messages act on a disk.

The BUS network is a linear transmission medium (bus) to which stations are attached. Any transmission from any station goes the length of the bus and can be received by all stations. TREE networks are simply bus networks with branches. Illustrations of BUS and TREE networks appear in Figure 13.

In BUS (or TREE) networks only one station can transmit at a time, and some type of access control must determine which station can transmit next. Often a protocol is shared among all stations; more rarely a centralized

Figure 13.
BUS and TREE Networks

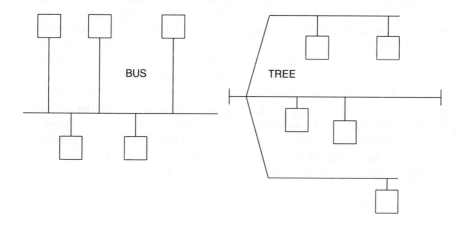

processor controls transmission sequence. Readers interested in a more detailed explanation of one implementation of such systems (IBM) are referred to Davis (1989).

Having been authorized to send, a station sends a packet with a destination address attached. The destination station recognizes its packets and copies them. Ethernet uses a straight-line cable with terminators on each end and computers attached to the bus cable at various points.

Some systems use a token-passing type of access, in which a "token" is passed from node to node in the system. Tokens are packets of information. Once a workstation has the token, it transforms the token into a "frame," adding the workstation address, the address of the workstation to receive the frame, and the information. The workstation then sends the frame of data. No other workstation can send during this time; each station simply passes the message along until it comes to the receiving station. At this point, a signal within the frame is changed to indicate receipt of the message. The frame of information continues until it arrives back at the sending workstation. The sending station then restores the original empty token and passes it to the nearest workstation.

If the reader looks at a token ring system, it will not look like a ring at all. Each workstation is connected to the system by a single cable containing two pairs of wires: one for transmission, one for receiving. The stations are all connected to a wiring concentrator which completes the ring.

In RING systems, every station receives the token and then regenerates it. If that node has information to transmit, the signal of the token is changed to a ZERO so that all subsequent nodes will know that information follows the token. When the token is passed to the node to which the information packet is addressed, that node captures the information in the packet, changing the signal of the token to indicate that the message has been read. When the originating node detects this switch, it reconverts the token into a free token and sends it on. The network nodes are now free to take the token and use it when it reaches each node. The nodes pass information to the nearest active node until the message reaches its destination. It resembles "an endless, circular version of the party game Telephone." (Glass, 1989)

Token systems have the advantage of giving one transmission between two stations priority. No matter how much information traffic there is, every node will have access to a token within some predetermined time span. There is also a down side: the delay while the token circulates through the system. The larger the system, the longer the delay. Also, in token passing systems, every node (workstation, PC) must be active. If a node goes down, the token cannot be read and retransmitted. Several companies have developed software to get around the "down-station" problem.

Other systems use a slotted-ring concept in which the ring connecting nodes is divided into area called "slots." When a node detects an empty slot, it may add an information packet into that slot. The receiving node reads each slot noting addresses. When an appropriately addressed packet appears, it is read, the "have read the packet" signal is changed, and the slot moves on. Slot sizes are fixed so that information packets are of uniform size.

Another access system is called "contention" access. In these systems, all stations compete for access to the channel. Carrier-sense multiple access (CSMA) is most commonly used. A station tests the system to see if anything is being transmitted. If no signal is detected, that station sends its message. If two packets contend for the channel, they may collide. Various companies have developed either collision-detection or collision-avoidance strategies to deal with this problem.

In collision detection, the sending node maintains contact with the channel to see its packet reach the destination node safely. If a collision is detected, the sending node emits a jam signal to all nodes, and the sending nodes stop packet sending. Collision-avoidance systems require a node test for a "free" channel before sending a packet and again just before the packet is transmitted. In these systems, collisions do not cut transmission. Instead, contending stations continue to send until their packets are received.

Each packet is assembled by the sending workstation and transmitted through the system to the receiving station. The length of the information field varies depending on the size of the information message and the number of packets required to send the entire message.

Standards for Communication in LANs

Creating a system in which information can be transferred efficiently and without loss of data requires standards. A number of national, governmental, and international organizations have been working on such standards during the 1980s. Standards for communication among computers must deal with a number of issues: (1) how a file of information is to be broken into small units for transmission and reassembled at the receiving computer, (2) how the receiving computer will check for lost or missing data from the file, (3) how to provide the computer with the ability to acknowledge when information has been received, (4) how to provide error detection, and (5) how the system will communicate with other systems.

In the multiple device system, a method must be established to control *when* a station may insert a packet. Usually this control is distributed throughout the system because each station has access logic that controls transmission and reception and indicates "busy" states. In the RING network, each station must have the ability to "packet" information and send and receive packets.

Almost all transmission systems (cables, etc.) have a capacity to carry more than a single digital signal. Such capability is called "multiplexing." To make such systems efficient, multiplexers have been developed so that systems carry multiple signals. Two common techniques for this process are frequency-division multiplexing (FDM) and time-division multiplexing (TDM). FDM uses the bandwidth of the medium to carry signals at different frequencies, much like FM radio. These carrier frequencies are surrounded by a specific bandwidth called a "channel." TDM systems separate signals through a timing system that allows interleaving of portions of signals in time. Here the sequence of time slots connected to a source is called a "channel" and one cycle of time slots is called a "frame."

Such multiplexing systems are used in telecommunications systems where computers are connected by combining signals from several computers and sending these packages over the telephone lines. The receiving computer separates these packages into their original sets. Multiplexers are used so that more than one machine can use a telephone line at the same time.

In local area networks, some form of error checking must be used so that the system is sure that messages have been received. All connected systems must have a set of conventions (protocols) to govern the format and control the information moving through the system. Generally protocols have two functions: contact and transfer of information. Most of the current systems have been developed in light of the Open Systems Interconnection Reference Model of the International Standards Organization. (Tannenbaum, 1981, and Stall, 1985)

The Open Systems Interconnect Model

For libraries and other information-sharing agencies, information resource sharing relies on *dependable* communication between computers. A number of technical, economic, and "people" problems have prevented easy communications between differing types of computers. Many software writers created programs to "convince" a distant computer that the computer attached by telephone was actually a terminal of the same brand as the host computer.

During recent years, attention has been paid to the problem of communication between computers by the International Standards Organization. This organization created a subcommittee named "Open Systems Interconnection (OSI)," which was assigned the job of developing a framework for the development of standards for computer-to-computer communication. The work of this subcommittee resulted in the Open Systems Interconnection Reference Model (OSI 7498). These standards are designed to be used by computer manufacturers and software developers so that the computers can be "open" to one another for communication.

Standards for local area networks derive from this Open Systems Interconnection Reference Model. The model combines the features found on commercial computer network architectures such as IBM's *SNA* and DEC's *Digital Network Architecture* (found in DNA/DEC-net). This seven-layered model allows each layer to support different functions without confusion. Figure 14 shows the layers of the OSI model.

The model allows communication only between adjacent layers which ensures the independence of each layer so that changes in one layer do not (necessarily) affect other layers. The model is rarely fully implemented. Many manufacturers of computers and network systems use proprietary systems and implement various functions at different layers. Many microcomputer communications packages for networking have not implemented all of these levels (or have combined several of them). Microcomputer networks often use only these layers: the physical link layer, the data-link layer, the session layer, and the file transfer layer. The network and transport layers come into play only when the microcomputers are connected into a local area network and the connection goes beyond simple file sharing.

For local area networks, the Institute of Electrical and Electronic Engineers (IEEE) through the 802 committee has developed a three-layer architecture corresponding to levels one and two of the OSI model. A list of American National Standards Institute/IEEE standards is found in the further-reading list at the end of this chapter. In the United States, the National Bureau of Standards, General Motors Corporation, and Boeing Computer Services have made a joint effort to implement the OSI model protocols.

The Network Advisory Committee and the Library of Congress Network Development and MARC Standards Office have opted to utilize the OSI model in the Linked Systems Project. In 1980 the Linked Authorities Telecommunications Group (OCLC, RLG, and the Library of Congress) decided to utilize the OSI model architecture to support communications for the Linked Systems Project (Davison, 1983). The Z39.50 standard for searching multiple bibliographic databases allows a user's query in a set of networks to be read and responded to by various bibliographic utilities. The user only types in one request. The standard assures a standard set of protocols for both the user's query and the utilities' database elements. The Linked Systems Project has tested the standard in a regional academic-library network in New York. If this standard can be implemented in a number of university-library and academic computer-communication networks, there is the potential for a nationwide online catalog for scholars. There remains the problem of linking this standard to the current protocols used by academic computer centers for on- and off-campus communications.

Figure 14.
The Open Systems Interconnection Reference Model Layers

(7) application—provides rules for specific tasks such as file transfer, sharing of programs, writing errors, database management, and network management

(6) presentation—puts data into forms that can be understood and manipulated by a human operator. Sends understandable data to screens and printers. Offers translation of varied computer codes (ASCII or EDCDIC) and terminal emulation. May provide for compacting, encoding, or decoding data.

(5) session—provides protocol to regulate how connections are made and terminated. Offers dialog control and message unit control.

(4) transport—regulates the communication session allowing computers to transmit data reliably and in sequence regardless of type of computer or physical location.

(3) network—routes messages through the communication system. Controls message flow in communications multiplexing so that one computer can communicate with several at the same time. This layer does error checking as well as message routing.

(2) link—establishes a channel of communication between computers and controls access to that channel. Protocol establishes instructions for the transmitting computer about how to frame the data in each message and about message sequencing. This layer may provide protocols for conversion of data by means of modems.

(1) physical—provides a set of rules governing physical connections in both electrical and mechanical terms

Gateways

Gateway processors are designed to connect two different networks (or network elements) together. These larger networks are often called Wide Area Networks (WANs). Almost all of these networks rely on some type of telephone common-carrier system for communication beyond the local building or area. An example would be the connection of a local area network to a public network (like TELENET, or TYMNET). Another example might be connecting the LAN to a mainframe.

Common carriers offer basic communication and transportation services to the public. When an individual using a workstation wants to use the local area network to contact remote systems, these companies lease communications services, add data-communication services, and charge for that service. Most of these services use the CCITT's X.25 interface standard for connecting the local computer to the public network. This standard covers the first three layers of the OSI standard. X.25 systems put information into addressed envelopes that are sent over telephone lines.

Many connected computers can "see" these envelopes, but only the computer to which the envelope is addressed can get at the contents. TYMNET, ACCUNET, and TIMEPLEX are three of the systems offering this service. Charges for such systems are based on two factors: (1) an access charge and (2) the amount of data (envelopes) sent. A full envelope costs the same amount as an envelope with only a little data, making X.25 systems expensive for libraries unless they are sending large-batch transmissions such as interlibrary-loan requests or acquisitions orders. (Graves and Clement, 1989)

For a workstation on a local area network to use public packet networks, there must be a means for the workstation or the local area network to provide X.25 format packets. Mainframe systems sometimes write their own software. Other options include leasing or buying certified X.25 PAD equipment. GTE-TELENET and TYMNET both allow for host-type connections for high-speed transmission and dial-up connections for lower-speed transmissions. It is possible to have a local area network serve as a host on these systems and to lease nodes to make the local area network into a full node on one of these systems. The decision about what kind of access to public channels is needed will be determined by the amount of data the library needs to transmit and the speed at which it needs that transmission.

It is much more expensive to establish a high-speed "permanent" connection than it is to dial up the service. But when lots of information is being transmitted, the cost of higher speed can be offset by lowering general communications costs and saving staff waiting time. For this reason, many large libraries doing a lot of communication with remote databases (like OCLC) use a high-speed leased line. Other libraries will use a dial-up service because their volume of communication does not justify the regular leased line and maintenance costs.

The higher-speed, more costly connections can be justified where databases are distributed among remote sites; where secure access at all times is essential; where some staff may be using the system from conferences, hotel rooms, or "in the field"; and where the response time of staff (to client inquiries) is critical.

Another alternative for relatively high-speed communications among computers over a wide area is digital dataphone service (DDS). Such systems support from 9,600 to 56,000 bits-per-second communication. Telephone companies offer such systems for about two hundred dollars a month per line. Several users may use the line at the same time. DDS systems provide very clean data transmission with a very low error rate.

Mobile data radio systems offer data communications utilizing FM radio signals. The Federal Communications Commission (FCC) regulates the use of these frequencies for any type of transmission. Two public service organizations can assist libraries in making an application for an FCC license:

APCO
  Box 280
  New Smyrna Beach, FL 32070
NABER (National Association of Business and Educational Radio)
  1501 Duke Street
  Alexandria, VA 22314

These data radio systems have a range of about twenty miles (line of sight). Because the performance of such systems depends so much on the terrain where the library is located, a study should be made of how the system can best operate at a specific site. One drawback of such systems is the high initial cost of equipment for towers, signal systems, repeaters, and connectors. A single-channel data radio costs about $4,000, and a system will require at least two of these radios. Antennas cost about $1,000 and usually must be mounted on a tower ($2,000 to $6,000). Other costs will include contractor fees (from feasibility study through installation and maintenance) and cabling. Equipment for a system will cost about $15,000.

Although initial equipment costs are high, operating costs are very low, and the data communication is high-quality and high-speed. The library also has the advantage of local ownership and control of the entire system (Brownrigg, 1985). When a library is sending data to a variety of remote sites (including bookmobiles) in a limited geographic area, such systems should be considered as an alternative to leased-line or dial-up communication services.

Broadband and Baseband LAN Systems

The architecture of local area networks can be divided into two types: broadband and baseband systems. Broadband systems have the advantage of allowing a single carrier to carry voice, image, and data over the carrier.

If one workstation is to deal with all forms of information—digital, voice, image—then broadband systems are the choice because they can handle all of these functions in one cable system. These systems arise out of the community-antenna television technology. To control signal variation, the cable television industry adopted broadband amplifiers to create a steady signal throughout the system.

This broadband technology provides a good communication channel that is relatively easy to split into separate channels. The 300 MHz cable can be split into fifty channels for data communication. Channels can be arranged directionally so that both inbound and outbound signals from the "head end" can be handled. Separate channels can be assigned to voice, video, and data, all at different transmission rates. All these factors—wide bandwidth, multiple channels, and higher data transfer rates—are reflected in a higher price. Standards for broadband media are being developed by the IEEE 802 committee. One major problem on the international scene is the difference between U.S. channel width (6 MHz) and European (8 MHz).

Examples of broadband systems are: Net/One (produced by Ungermann-Bass) uses a broadband system in which inbound signals are carried at 59.75 to 89.75 MHz, and outbound signals are carried at 252 to 282 MHz. Five channels of information are carried each way at up to 5 Mbps. The system uses an RF modem that can connect up to 24 nodes using RS232, IEEE488, RS449, or V.35 serial standards. The system will also operate on Ethernet baseband or fiber-optic cable. LocalNet (produced by Sytek) uses 40 to 106 MHz for inbound signals and 196 to 262 MHz for outbound signals. The System 20 allows 128 Kbps transmission speed which is acceptable for low-speed, low-traffic systems utilizing personal computers.

Baseband systems are less expensive and slower. Typical baseband systems will be cabled with twisted wire cable and transmit between 0 and 10 Mbps. Possible problems with baseband systems include noise, lack of integration of voice and image transmission, and a limitation on the number of workstations. In library local area networks which are to focus on digital information transfer *within a limited area*, the baseband solution may be sufficient. Baseband systems run into difficulty when the LAN must be interconnected with other systems and go beyond digital transmission.

A baseband system puts a digital signal on the cables wired between components of the system. The system has only one path no matter what cable (medium) is used for transmission of data. At a speed of 10 Mbps the distance between units is about 500 meters. Repeaters (devices which clean up the signal and strengthen it) can increase the distance to 1.5 kilometers. Usually transmission is TDM and there are no frequencies to separate.

One example of a baseband system is Omninet, produced by Corvus Systems, which carries up to 1 Mbps over 300 meters, serving up to 64 nodes.

Repeaters can lengthen this distance to 4,000 feet. If there is a signal collision, each workstation waits a random amount of time before trying to send a signal again. Increased data traffic on the cables causes longer and longer wait states. Omninet uses a transporter interface to take each node's information, puts it in packets, and transmits it. The transporter interface has direct access to the memory of each workstation. This direct memory access (DMA) increases memory access speed. Omninet utilizes an Advanced Data Link Controller for collision avoidance among data transmissions. The system uses a "Reliable Datagram" for sending and receiving messages.

Another popular example of such systems is Ethernet which was developed by Xerox with the backing of Digital Equipment Corporation and Intel Corporation. Ethernet carries data at a 10Mbps rate, and sections can be 1,600 feet long. With repeaters, this distance can be extended to 2.3 kilometers. Ethernet contains only the first two layers of the ISO standard (physical and link layers). The developers and other manufacturers supply implementation of the other layers. The list of systems in appendix B notes whether Ethernet can be implemented in a particular system.

Cables for LANs

The type of cable used in the network affects the speed and cost of the system. The slowest cables are twisted-pair cables. Coaxial cable is faster, harder to work with, and more expensive. Fiber-optic cable is very secure and efficient but also more expensive.

Fiber-optic is the newest cable technology. Bryce (1989, p. 253) describes optic fiber as being "made by drawing a large glass, called a 'prefrom' out over a long distance until it is one long piece of pure glass whose diameter is measured in millionths of a meter: microns." Fiber-optic cables have two parts: a core and a cover called a "cladding." Light signals pass through the core, and the cladding refracts (bends) the light back into the core. The whole cable is covered by chemical coatings and a plastic covering. In local area networks, light signals from LED devices send light signals down the cable to the receiving site.

When compared with the metal cables, fiber optics have a number of advantages:

the data rate of the cable. Fiber optics can carry a signal at 1,000 megabits per second.
the resistance to interference. Many forms of static and electric signals cannot penetrate the optical-fiber system.

the lack of signal distortion and very low error rate. Fiber optics maintain
excellent signals over the cable with very low error rates.

the security of the cable system from intrusion. Fiber optic cables are
difficult to tap and do not radiate signals like metallic cables.

resistance to explosion. Fiber cables do not have the spark potential of
metal cables. Since they have no metal parts, lightning damage is less
likely.

smaller and lighter cables

Many institutions have telephone systems that do not use two of the wires
in the four-wire cables for telephone purposes. If there is no current in these
lines, they can be adapted for a baseband local area network. Coaxial cable
is often recommended because of its resistance to noise interference and its
capacity. However, coaxial cable is more difficult to string and must not be
placed on the floor since it must not be abraded, severed, crushed, or
shorted. Figure 15 lists cable selection options.

Conclusion

The library manager cannot be expected to know all of the equipment or
technical-standards details surrounding workstations and local area networks. However, as Flower (1988, p. 27) notes: "Sooner or later, many of us
will have to determine precisely what hardware to buy. Knowledge of current
industry trends and likely future developments can only help to simplify
decisions that may involve thousands of dollars." Certain guidelines do
apply to all librarians:

(1) read the relevant library literature on library microcomputing and
local area networks. Include in that reading the materials collected
from vendors at library association exhibits.

(2) when you go to exhibits (library or industry) ask lots of questions.
Know what your *use* requirements are.

(3) visit libraries and other agencies which have installed local area
networks and used workstations. Do not forget local educational
institutions (public schools, community colleges, and universities) in
arranging visits.

(4) consider several vendors of software and equipment. Unless you have
a resident guru of computers and telecommunications do not order a
local area network or workstation by mail.

(5) be prepared for the planning, technical installation, and trouble-
shooting stages to last longer than you expected.

Figure 15.
Choosing a Cable Type

(Check)

(1) Must it be simple to install and very rugged? _____

(2) Do you need the highest possible data transfer rate? _____

(3) Do you need to couple inexpensive installation with distances up to one kilometer? _____

(4) Do you need to couple inexpensive installation with distances from one to ten kilometers? _____

(5) Must you reduce fire hazards in the workplace? _____

(6) Do you want ease of adding, subtracting, and moving workstations? _____

(7) Do you have a large area to connect? _____

(8) Do you need high security from wiretaps and other assaults on the physical medium? _____

(9) Will you use STAR architecture? _____

(10) Will you use token-passing RING or CSMA/CD BUS? _____

(11) Do you need multidrop capacity? _____

(12) Do you need better-than-average freedom from radio frequency (RF) and other (EMI) interference, or lightning-caused power surges? _____

If you checked 1,3,6,9,10, and 11, consider twisted-wire cable
If you checked 1,4,6,9,10, and 11, consider baseband coax
If you checked 2,5,8,12, and 9 or 10, consider fiber optics
If you checked 7 but not 9, consider a microwave link for the interbuilding part of your data path.

(Marney-Petix, 1986, p. 100)

Further Reading

This listing provides detailed and technical information on standards and various operational applications of those standards by producers of local area networks and workstations.

Standards

IEEE Standard 802.2-1985. *Local area network (Logical Link Control).* (No. DQ 943). IEEE Computer Society, 10662 Los Vaqueros Circle, Los Alamitos, Calif.

IEEE Standard 802.3-1985. *Local area network (Carrier Sense Multiple Access with Collision Detection—CSMA/DD).* (No. DQ 942)

IEEE Standard 802.4-1985. *Local area network (Token Passing Bus Access Method and Physical Layer Specifications).* (No. DQ 938)

IEEE Standard 802.5-1985. *Local area network (Token Ring Access Method and Physical Layer Specifications).* (No. DQ 939)

International Standards Organization. Technical Committee 97. Subcommittee 16. (March 1978). *Provisional model of open systems architecture.* (Doc. N34) Geneva, Switz.

———. (June 1979). *Reference model of open systems architecture.* (Doc. N227)

OSI

Aschenbrenner, J. R. 1987. Open systems interconnection. *IBM Systems Journal* 25 (3-4): 369-79.

Beach, B., et al. 1985. OSI protocols link PC-DOS, XENIX and IRMA. *Systems and Software* 4 (3): 89-95.

Becker, J. T. Open systems free users from their mainframe architecture. *Data Communications* 16 (2): 167-70.

Bhabuta, L. 1986. Standards and systems development—A practical approach to standardization. *Data Processing* 28 (7): 344-50.

Bicknell, D. 1987. What lies behind the legend of OSI? *Computer News* (June 4, 1987): 4.

Bono, P. R. 1986. The standards process. *IEEE Computer Graphics and Applications* 6 (8): 12-16.

Bozzotti, M. 1986. The impact of new technologies, what kind of evolution for the reference model? In *Open systems 1986.* Pinner, Middlesex, Eng.: Online Publications.

Campbell-Grant, I. R. 1986. Open systems application layer standards for text and office systems. *Journal of the Institution of Electronic and Radio Engineers* 56 (6-7): 233-36.

Carson, G. S. 1986. The reference model for computer graphics. *IEEE Computer Graphics and Applications* 6 (8): 17-23.

Cheetham, C. J. 1986. The protocols of open networks. *Communications* 3 (2): 32-34.

Denenberg, R. 1985. Open systems interconnection. *Library Hi Tech* 3 (1, Issue 9): 15-26.

Des Jardins, R., and Foley, J. S. 1984. Open systems interconnection: A review and status report. *Journal of Telecommunication Networks* 3 (3): 194-209.

Duc, N. Q., and Chew, E. K. 1985. ISDN protocol architecture. *IEEE Communications Magazine* 23 (3): 15-22.

Foley, J. 1985. Standards. The status and directions of open systems. *Data Communications* 14 (2): 177-93.

Folts, H. C., and Des Jardins, R., Eds. 1983. Open systems interconnection (OSI)—New international standards architecture and protocols for distributed information systems. *Proceedings of IEEE* 71 (13): 1331-1452.

Fong, E. N., and Jefferson, D. K. 1986. Reference model for standardization. *Computer standards and interfaces* 5 (7): 93-98.

Freeman, H. A., and Thurber, K. J. 1985. *Tutorial: Local network equipment.* Los Angeles, Calif.: Computer Society of the IEEE.

Gilhooly, D. OSI—After the seventh level. *Telecommunication* 21 (2): 48-54.

Heywood, P. 1987. ISO plans cure for incompatible versions of OSI standards: ISPs. *Data Communications* 16 (9): 68.

International open systems 87. 1987. Middlesex. Eng.: Online Publications.

The ISDN and its impact on information technology. 1986. IEEE Conference Publication No. 244.

Jacobsen, T., and Thisted, P. 1980. CCITT recommendation X.25 as part of the OSI reference model of open system interconnection. *Computer Communications Review* 10 (1-2): 48-55.

Jenkins, P. A., and Knightson, K. G. Open systems interconnection—an introductory guide. *British Telecommunications Engineering* 3 (2): 86-91.

Kearsey, B., and Jones, W. T. 1985. International standardisation in telecommunications and information processing. *Electronics and Power* 31 (9): 643-51.

Larmouth. J. 1985. OSI enters the implementation phase. *Data Processing* 27 (1): 11-14.

Longman, T. C. 1985. Open architecture internetworking. In *LOCALNET 85: Proceedings of a conference, New York.* London: Online International Ltd.

Malde, S. 1986. Message handling standards. *Computer Communications,* 9 (2): 79-85.

Mantelman, L. 1987. Appletalk sheds its image as a "wimpy" network. *Data Communications* 16 (3): 60,70,72,76.

Marsden, B. 1986. *Communication network protocols.* Bromley, Kent, Eng.: Chartwell-Bratt.

Mayne, A. J. 1986. *Linked local area networks.* 2nd ed. New York: Wiley and Sons.

Meijer, A. 1986. Systems network architecture (SNA) and open system interconnection (OSI). In *Communication standards; State of the art report 14:3.* Ed. A. V. Stokes. Maidenhead, Berkshire, Eng.: Pergamon Infotech, 155–64.

Melendez, W., and Petersen, E. L. 1986. The upper layers of the ISO/OSI reference model (part I). *Computer Standards and Interfaces* 5 (1) 13–46. (Part II is in 5 (2): 65–77)

Mills, K. L. Testing OSI protocols: NBS advances the state of the art. *Data Communications* 13 (3): 277–96.

Nemeth, K. 1985. Principles of the document interchange protocol for CCITGT telematic services. *IEEE Communications Magazine* 23 (3): 23–28.

O'Mara, R. 1985. OSI—The open system interface of "the building block of the 80s." *LASIE* 26 (3): 2–5.

Open systems: Development and applications. 1986. Middlesex, Eng.: Online Publications.

Open systems 1986. 1986. Middlesex, Eng.: Online Publications.

O'Reilly, D. 1986. Knitting together X.25, Ethernet, UNIX and Mainframe. *Data Communications* 15 (9): 179–92.

OSI. The OSI handbook: Questions and answers. 1987. London: ICL Press Ltd.

PC communications get in on the OSI act. 1985. *Systems and Software* 4 (5): 65–78.

Piscitello, D. M., et. al., 1986. Internetworking in an OSI environment. *Data Communications* 15 (5): 118–36.

Rout, T. J. SNA to OSI. 1987. *Data Communications* 16 (5): 120–38.

Rutowski, A. M. 1987. Open network architecture: An introduction. *Telecommunications* 21 (2): 28,30,37–38,40,46.

Schindler, S. 1981. Open systems, today and tomorrow. A personal perspective. *Computer Networks* 5 (3): 162–76.

SNA and OSI: Living together. *Datamation* 33 (1): 92–97 to 97–110.

Speikernell, D. G. 1986. The role of international standards in removing barriers to trade and assisting developing countries. *International Journal of Technology Management* 1 and 2: 197–208.

Stallings, W. 1985. *Computer communications, architecture, protocols and standards.* Los Angeles, Calif.: Institute of Electrical and Electronic Engineers, Computer Society Press.

Stallings, W. Standards: The new fibre diet. *Datamation* 33 (6): 61–64.

Stamper, D. 1986. *Business data communications*. Reading, Mass.: Addison-Wesley.

Stokes, A. V. 1987. Protocol specification and verification. *Communicate* 7 (2): 6 and 7 (3): 8.

Straus, P. 1987. OSI throughput performance: Breakthrough or bottleneck? *Data Communications* 16 (5): 53–56.

Sundstrom, R. J., et al. 1987. SNA: Current requirements and direction. *IBM Systems Journal* 26 (1): 13–36.

Thompson, D. M. 1986. LAN management standards—Architecture and protocols. In *Proceedings of the IEEE INFOCOM 1986*, pp. 355–63.

Underwood, S. 1987. ISDN on trial. *Datamation* 33 (February 1): 52–56.

VAX OSI Tranport Service (VOTS) V1.1—The path to successful multivendor networking. 1986. Digital Equipment Corporation, Brochure ED 29014–42.

Wang, B., and Hutchinson, D. 1987. Protocol testing techniques. *Computer Communications* 10 (2): 79–87.

Weissberger, A. J., and Israel, J. E. 1987. What the new internetworking standards provide. *Data Communications* 16 (2): 141–56.

——. 1987. Communicating between heterogeneous networks. *Data Communications* 16 (3): 215–35.

Whittle, B. S. 1985. Standards for the evolving ISDNs: Progress and challenges: A road map. *Computer Communications Review* 15 (3): 50–64.

Witt, M. 1986. Moving the DoD to OSI protocols: A first step. *Computer Communications Review* 16 (2): 2–7.

Library-Related Articles

Bigelow, L., and Calabrese, A. 1989. Libraries and telecommunications technologies. *College & Research Libraries News* 50 (March): 195–99.

Boss, R. W. 1985. The open systems architecture as a building block in a health sciences information network. *Bulletin of the Medical Library Association* 73 (4): 330–37.

First ISO/OSI inter-library transfer of bibliographic records successful. 1986. *Database and Network Journal* 16 (3): 5.

Flower, E., and L. Thustrup. 1988. Setting up a public use local area network. *Wilson Library Bulletin* 63 (September): 45–47.

Hill, L. L. 1985. Issues on network participation for corporate librarians. *Special Libraries* 76 (Winter): 2–10.

Lynch, C. A., and Brownrigg, E. B. 1986. The telecommunications landscape: 1986. *Library Journal* 111 (October 1): 40–46.

Nyren, K. 1985. California conference on networking: First steps taken to mobilize state's library communities to build statewide multitype network. *Library Journal* 110 (November 15): 12–14.

A

Producers of Workstations

Apollo Computer, Inc.
330 Billerica Rd.
Chelsford, MA 01824
(617-256-6600)

Offers Model DN3000-L with 12.5 MHz Motorla 680201 CPU and a 68881 floating point coprocessor, 4 megabytes of RAM, 72-megabyte hard disk. Utilizes Apollo token ring or Ethernet network connections, windowing interface, Domain version of Unix and Aegis network software. $7,690 (Summer 1988). Model DN3000-C is an enhanced version for $11,600.

Apple Computer, Inc.
20525 Mariani Ave.
Cupertino, CA 95014
(408-996-1010)

Offers Macintosh II, 15.7 MHz Motorola 68020 CPU, 68881 floating point coprocessor, 1 megabyte RAM, 40-megabyte hard disk and desktop bus ports, as well as one SCSI port. $6,396.

Compaq Computer Corporation
20555 FM 149
Houston, TX 77070
(713-370-7040)

Offers Deskpro 386/20 Model 60 with 20 MHz Intel 80386 CPU, socket for coprocessor, 1 megabyte of RAM, 32K statis RAM cache, 1.2-megabyte floppy-disk drive, 60-megabyte hard disk. $7,853.

Digital Equipment Corporation
146 Main St
Maynard, MA 01754
(617-897-5111)

133

Offers Vaxstation 2000 workstation with Microvax II CPU and floating point unit, 4 megabytes RAM, built-in Ethernet controller, 1.2-megabyte floppy-disk drive, 42-megabyte hard disk, software licenses for VMS or Unix operating system, network software, windowing interfacing, and several programming languages. DEC maintains a 16,000-workstation network worldwide. $7,650–$10,950.

IBM Corporation
Old Orchard Road
Armonk, NY 10504
(914-765-1900)

Offers PS/2 Model 80-071 personal-computer system with 16MHz Intel 80386 CPU, socket for coprocessor, 21 megabytes of RAM, 1.44-megabyte floppy-disk drive, 70-megabyte hard drive. $9,180.

Sun Microsystems, Inc.
2550 Garcia Ave.
Mountain View, CA 94043
(415-960-1300)

Offers Sun 3/50M-4 workstation with 15MHz Motorola 68020 CPU, 4 megabytes of RAM, 72-megabyte hard disk, built in Ethernet connection, software licenses for SunOS (a Unix machine), windowing interface, network software, and several programming languages. $7,963. A faster processor, the Sun 3/60FC-4 workstation is offered for $11,789.

B

Network Characteristics

A number of companies produce low cost peer-to-peer networks which may serve many library needs. The following table lists some of the characteristics of such networks.

Peer-to-Peer LANS

Product	Company	Micros Compatible	DOS-Supported	Memory for Network	Maximum Stations	Network Hardware	Gateways	Software Price	Hardware Price
ZeroLAN	Applied Knowledge Group	PC	yes	48K	6	RS232, RJ11	none	$149 per node	included
ZeroNET	"	PC	yes NetBIOS	48K	10	RS232	none	$299 per node	included
Network OS	CBIS	PC	yes NetBIOS	60K 148K for fileserver	30	NetBIOS NetBIOS	SNA3270	$160 per node	
Grapevine	Computer Pathways	PC	yes NetBIOS	126K	50	Grapevine adapter	none	$595 per node	included
PC/NOS	Corvus Systems	PC	yes NetBIOS	184K	64	OmniNET adapter	SNA3270	$695 per 64 node	$149 per node
NetCommander	Digital Products	PC	yes NetBIOS	240K	32	RS232 NetHub	SNA3270	$150 per node	$2,950 per hub (16 nodes)
DNA Network	DNA Network	PC	yes NetBIOS	100K	64	DNA	SNA3270	$695 per 64 nodes	
EasyNet 116	EasyNet Systems	PC	yes NetBIOS	150K	250	EasyNet adapter	bridge	$300 per node	included
EasyNet II	"	PC	yes NetBIOS	150K	2	RS232	bridge	$114 per 2-node system	
EasyNet NOS	"	PC	yes NetBIOS	55K 65K for fileserver	250	RS232 Ethernet ARCnet Tokenring	SNA2370	$795 for up to 16 nodes	

Product	Company	Computer	OS	Memory	Max nodes	Adapter	Topology	Price (server/network)	Price per node
K-NOS	Kimtrom	PC	yes NetBIOS	80K 160K for fileserver	20	XL100, ARCnet Ethernet Tokenring	bridge	$599 for 30 modes	$299 per node
D-Link	LocalNet Communications	PC	yes NetBIOS	50K	255	D-link adapter	SNA2370	$95	$249 per node
vLAN+	Networth	PC	yes NetBIOS	140K 380K for fileserver	64	vLAN adapter	SNA2370 Tokenring Ethernet	$595 per node	$249 per node
PCnet	Orchid Technology	PC	yes NetBIOS	128K	255	PCnet adapter	none	$1,090 per 2-node network	$495 per node
QNX	Quantum Software Systems	PC	guest OS	145K	255	ARCnet adapter	none	$1,800 per 18-node network	$495 per node
EasyLAN	Server Technology	PC	yes NetBIOS	20K	18	RS232	bridge	$99 per node	
Simple-NET OnePlus	Simple-NET Systems	PC	yes NetBIOS	200K	256	Simple-NET adapter	SNA3270	$175 per node	included
LANlink 5x	The Software Link	PC	yes NetBIOS	20K per station 38K for fileserver	17	RS232	SNA3270	$275 per server $125 per node	
SummaNet	Summa Computer Systems	PC	guest OS	100K	2,000	ARCnet adapter	SNA3270 Ethernet	$995 per 4 nodes	$495 per node
NetWare 286	Televideo Systems (note: Televideo also sells an 8 node system for $795)	PC	yes NetBIOS	41K per station 512K for fileserver	100	RS232 ARCnet EtherNet	Ethernet ARCnet Tokenring	$2,195 per network	$199 per node
10Net	10Net Communications	PC	guest OS NetBIOS	117K	32	PCnet TokenRing	Tokenring	$695 per node	$395

Product	Company	Micros Compatible	DOS-Supported	Memory for Network	Maximum Stations	Network Hardware	Gateways	Software Price	Hardware Price
TOPS/DOS	TOPS	PC	yes	120K per station 80K for fileserver	32	TOPS Flashcard, Appletalk	yes	$189 per node	$239 per node
TOPS/Macintosh	"	Mac		98K	32		yes	$249 per node	
Tapestry/3	Torus Systems	PC	yes	85K per station 150K for fileserver	8	NetBIOS	SNA3270	$795 per 8 nodes	
Net-127	Trans-M	PC	yes	32K	127	Net127 adapter	3Com Novell	$249 per node	included
Waterloo	Waterloo Micro	PC	guest OS	122 per 256K for fileserver	255	ARCnet Tokenring	SNA3270	$2495 per 25 nodes	$345 per node
ViaNet 3.06	Western Digital	PC	yes	140K per station 140K for fileserver	255	StarLAN Ethernet	none	$99 per node	$259 per node
PC Share	Zaki	PC	yes NetBIOS	10K per station 4K for fileserver	9	RS232 SHAREplus adapter	SNA3270	$995 per node	

Local Area Network
Manufacturers

Alloy Computer Products Inc.
100 Pennsylvania Ave.
Framingham, MA 01701
(617-875-6100)

Cartridge tape drives and backup systems, NTNX operating system. Founded: 1979.

Applied Knowledge Groups, Inc.
1095 E. Duane Ave. Suite 203
Sunnyvale, CA 94086
(408-739-0300)

Software for information retrieval and data communications. Founded: 1983.

Banyan Systems, Inc.
115 Flanders Rd.
Westboro, MA 01581
(617-898-1000)

VINES, a local network operating system. Also offers several networking systems that integrate local and remote PCs into clusters. Founded: 1983.

Cincinnati Bell Information System, Inc.
5875 Peachtree Industrial Blvd.
Building 100, Suite 170
Norcross, GA 30092
(404-446-1332)

Network OS operating system. Cards for a variety of LAN systems. Founded: 1978.

Computer Pathways
19102 North Creek Parkway
Bothell, WA 98011
(206-487-1000)

Local area network products. Founded: 1984.

Corvus Systems, Inc.
160 Great Oaks Blvd.
San Jose, CA 95119-1347
(408-281-4100)

Components for network-based systems. Founded: 1979.

Digital Products, Inc.
108 Water St.
Watertown, MA 02172
(617-924-1680)

Peripheral sharing devices and network products. Founded: 1984

DNA Network, Inc.
81 Great Valley Parkway
Malvern, PA 19355
(215-296-7420)

Networking communication products and DNA Network. Founded: 1978.

EasyNet Systems, Inc.
4283 Village Center Court
Mississauga, Ontario, Canada L4Z 1S2
(416-273-6410)

Kimtron Corp.
1709 Junction Court
Building 380
San Jose, CA 95112
(408-436-6550)

Video display terminals and local area network-based intelligent workstations and diskless micros. Founded: 1979.

LocalNet Communications Inc.
3303 Harbor Blvd.
Suite E8
Costa Mesa, CA 92626
(714-549-7942)

Local area network products. Founded: 1986.

Netline Inc.
85 W. Center St.
P.O. Box 3000
Provo, UT 84603
(801-337-6000)

Network products for small business. Founded: 1986.

NetWorth Inc.
8101 Ridgepoint Drive
Suite 107
Irving, TX 75063
(214-869-1331)

Networking products that can be installed on existing telephone wiring. Founded: 1985.

Norvell Inc.
122 E. 1770 S.
Provo, UT 84601
(801-379-5900)

Local area networks and data-communication products including *Advanced NetWare* and *SFT NetWare*. Founded: 1983.

Orchid Technology, Inc.
45365 Northport Loop West
Fremont, CA 94538
(415-683-0300)

PCnet LAN, graphics adapters, accelerator cards, and multifunction cards. Founded: 1982.

Quantum Software Systems, Ltd.
175 Terrence Mathews Crescent
Kanata, Ontario, Canada K2M 1W8
(613-591-0931)

QNX peer-to-peer operating system with distributed processing and distributed file systems.

Server Technology Inc.
140 Kifer Court
Sunnyvale, CA 94086
(800-835-1515)

Local area networking for PCs. Founded: 1984.

Simple-NET Systems
(Division of BCSoft Corp)
544 West Lambert Rd.
Suite A
Brea, CA 92621
(714-526-5151)

Three turnkey LAN systems. Founded: 1986.

Summa Computer Systems
215 E. Water St.
Syracuse, NY 13202
(315-475-0870)

SummaNet network operating system. Founded: 1983.

Televideo Systems Inc.
1170 Morse Ave.
P.O. Box 3586
Sunnyvale, CA 94088-3586
(408-745-7760)

Video display monitors, local area networks, PC-compatible business systems, and printers. Founded: 1977.

10Net Communications Inc.
(Division of Digital Communications Associates, Inc.)
7016 Corporate Way
Dayton, OH 45459
(513-433-2238)

Local area network; 10Base, a database management system; 10Net SNA Gateway, linking LANs to IBM mainframe computers. Formerly Fox Research Inc.

The Software Link Inc.
3577 Parkway Lane
Norcross, GA 30092
(404-448-5465)

LANlink, PC Emulink, PC-MOS/386 network multiuser, multitask products. Founded: 1983.

3Com Corp.
3165 Kifer Road
Santa Clara, CA 95052
(408-562-6400)

Network systems including interface cards and network operating systems. Founded: 1979.

TOPS
(A Sun Microsystems Inc. Company)
950 Marina Village Parkway
Alameda, CA 94501
(415-769-9669)

Variety of networking and communications products for PC and Macintosh environments. Founded: 1984.

Torus Systems Inc.
240B Twin Dophon Drive
Redwood City, CA 94065
(415-594-9336)

Local area networking, gateways, and file servers, related software and communications products. Founded: 1984.

Trans-M Corp.
28 Blacksmith Drive
Medfield, MA 02052
(617-359-5144)

Intelligent RS232 connector, NET-127 network software package. Founded: 1986.

Traveling Software Inc.
19310 N. Creek Parkway
Bothell, WA 98011
(206-487-1284)

Productivity software for laptop PCs. Founded: 1982.

Ungermann-Bass Inc.
3900 Freedom Circle
Santa Clara, CA 95054
(408-496-0111)

Networking products for the PC. Net/One operating system, bridges, gateways to mainframes. Founded: 1979.

Univation Inc
638 Gibraltar Court
Milpitas, CA 95035
(408-263-1200)

Local area network products, desktop publishing systems, expansion boards, and mass storage devices. Founded: 1983.

Waterloo Microsystems Corp.
3597 Parkway Lane
Suite 200
Norcross, GA 30092
(404-441-9252)

Network communication systems. PORT is a multitasking PC LAN with links to mainframe computers. Founded: 1982.

Western Digital Corp.
2445 McCabe Way
Irvine, CA 92714
(714-863-0102)

Disk-storage equipment, communications, and image systems. Founded: 1970.

White Crane Systems Inc.
6889 Peachtree Industrial Blvd.
Suite 151
Norcross, GA 30092
(404-394-3119)

Connectivity products and business-utility software for microcomputers.

Zaki Corp.
Maple Technology Park
420 Maple St.
Marlboro, MA 01752
(617-480-0201)

PC add-on products. PC Share and PC Shareplus Local are network systems. Founded: 1984.

B I B L I O G R A P H Y

Alberico, R. 1988. Workstations for reference and retrieval: Part one: The scholar's workstation. *Small Computers in Libraries* March, 8 (3): 4–10.

American Society of Safety Engineers. 1985. *Workstation design for current office environments*. Des Plaines, Ill.: The Society.

Andriole, S. J. 1985. *The future of information processing technology*. Princeton: Petrocelli Books.

Anderla, G., and Dunning, A. 1987. *Computer strategies 1990–9: Technologies, costs, markets*. Chichester, Eng.: John Wiley & Sons.

Association of Data Processing Service Organizations. 1985. *Sample corporate policies on software piracy*. Arlington, Va.: ADAPSO.

Association of Research Libraries. 1985. *Microcomputer software policies in ARL libraries* (SPEC Kit No. 123). Washington, D.C.: ARL.

Brod, C. 1984. *Technostress: The human cost of the computer revolution*. Menlo Park, Calif.: Addison-Wesley.

Brownrigg, E. 1985. Wide-area networks. In Culotta, W.; Ercegovac, Z.; and Roth, D., *Local area networks and libraries: The Los Angeles Chapter of ASIS seminar proceedings*. Studio City, Calif.: Pacific Information, Inc., 62–72.

Bryce, J. Y. 1989. Fiber vs. metal. *Byte* 14 (1): 253–58.

Camarado, L. 1988. Raymond Walters College at the University of Cincinnati. In *Developing microcomputer work areas in academic libraries*, ed. J. Uppgard. Westport, Conn.: Meckler, 30–37.

Chorafas, D. M. 1984. *Designing and implementing local area networks*. New York: McGraw-Hill.

Cimbala, D. J. 1985. There goes the neighborhood. *Technicalities*, 5 (6): 9.

Curtis, H. 1988. The scholar's workstation: Networking on campus. *Wilson Library Bulletin* 63 (October): 46–51.

Dakshinamurti, G. B. 1985. Automation's effect on library personnel. *Canadian Library Journal* 42 (December): 343–51.

Davis, R. 1989. A logical choice. *Byte* 14 (January): 309–15.

Davison, W. 1983. The WLN/RLG/LC Linked Systems Project. *Information Technology and Libraries* 2 (March): 34–46.

DeBuse, R. 1988. So that's a book . . . Advancing technology and the library. *Information Technology and Libraries* 7 (March): 7–18.

Dewey, P. R. 1984. *Public access microcomputers; A handbook for librarians*. White Plains, N.Y.: Knowledge Industry Publications.

———. 1988. Looking at review sources. In Hannigan, J. A., and Intner, S.S., *The library microcomputer environment*. Phoenix, Ariz.: Oryx Press, 63–76.

Dubin, E., and Kuhner, R. 1986. Use of microcomputers in library instruction. *Resource sharing and information networks* 3 (Fall–Winter): 65–82.

Duke, J. K., and Hirshon, A. 1986. Policies for microcomputers in libraries: An administrative model. *Information Technology and Libraries* 5 (September): 193–203.

Emmett, A., and Gabel, D. 1986. *Direct connections; Making your personal computer communicate.* New York: New American Library.

Flower, E. 1988. The Workstation market. *Wilson Library Bulletin* 63 (October): 24–27.

Futas, E. 1988. Collection use: Reference work with hardware and software. In Hannigan, J. A., and Intner, S. S. *The library microcomputer environment.* Phoenix, Ariz.: Oryx Press, 45–60.

Glass, B. 1989. Hands on under the hood: The token ring. *Byte* 14 (January): 363–76.

Grandjean, E., et al. 1983. Constraining postures at office workstations. In *Ergonomics of workstation design*, ed. T. O. Kvalseth. London: Butterworths, 19–27.

Graves, R., and Clement, R. 1989. Telecommunications: a primer for librarians. *Wilson Library Bulletin* 63 (5): 50–52.

Hannigan, J. A. 1988. An expanded managerial role in a microcomputer environment. In Intner, S.S., and Hannigan, J. A., *The library microcomputer environment: Management issues.* Phoenix, Ariz.: Oryx Press.

Hunting, W., et al. 1980a. Constrained posture in accounting machine operators. *Applied Ergonomics* 11: 145–49.

———. 1980b. Constraining postures of VDT operators. In *Ergonomic aspects of visual display terminals*, ed. E. Grandjean and E. Vigliani. London: Taylor and Francis, 175–81.

Hutchins, R. M. 1947. The administrator. In *Works of the mind*, ed. R. B. Heywood. Chicago: University of Chicago Press, 135–56.

International Standards Organization. Technical Committee 97. Subcommittee 16. 1978. *Provisional model of open systems architecture.* (Doc. N34, March) Geneva: The organization.

———. 1979. *Reference model of open systems architecture.* (Doc. N227, June) Geneva: The organization.

Intner, S. S. 1988. Developing software collections. In Hannigan, J. A., and Intner, S. S. *The library microcomputer environment.* Phoenix, Ariz.: Oryx Press, 3–21.

Kemper, M. 1988. Local area networking: The management problem. In Intner, S. S., and Hannigan, J. A. *The library microcomputer environment: Management issues.* Phoenix, Ariz.: Oryx Press, 187–206.

Kenney, D., and Wilson, L. 1988. Online catalogs: Some ergonomic considerations. *Wilson Library Bulletin* 63 (September): 46–48.

Kleeman, M., et al. 1987. *PC LAN primer.* Indianapolis, Ind.: Howard W. Sams & Co.

Lynch, C. A., and Brownrigg, E. B. 1986. The telecommunications landscape: 1986. *Library Journal* 111 (October 1): 40–46.

McKirdy, P. A. 1988. Copyright issues for microcomputer collections. In Hannigan, J. A., and Intner, S.S. *The library microcomputer environment*. Phoenix, Ariz.: Oryx Press, 96–125.

MacLean, P. 1988. State University of New York at Geneseo. In *Developing microcomputer work areas in academic libraries*, ed. J. Uppgard. Westport, Conn.: Meckler, 17–28.

Marmion, D. 1988. State-of-the-art library workstations: A guided tour. *Wilson Library Bulletin* 63 (October): 28–33.

Marney-Petix, V. 1986. *Networking and data communication for business.* Englewood Cliffs, N.J.: Prentice-Hall.

Miller, R. B. 1983. Radiation, ergonomics, ion depletion, and VDTs: Healthful use of visual display terminals. *Information Technology and Libraries* 2(2): 151–58.

———. 1986. Radiation, ergonomics, ion depletion, and VDTs: Healthful use of visual display terminals. In *Training issues in changing technology*. Chicago: Library Administration and Management Association, American Library Association, 27–44.

Miller, W., and Gratch, B. 1989. Making connections: Computerized reference services and people. *Library Trends* 37 (4): 387–401.

Nelson, N. M. 1988. Library workstations: A survey of available hardware and software options. *Library Technology Reports* 24 (January–February): 5–24.

Nordgren, L. The Macintosh as a library workstation: Some significant advantages. *Wilson Library Bulletin* 63 (October): 35–41, 118.

Online Computer Library Center. 1987. *Communications and access planning guide.* Dublin, Ohio: OCLC.

———. 1987. *Planning guide supplement.* Dublin, Ohio: OCLC.

Peischl, T. M., and Montgomery, M. 1986. Back to the warehouse or some implications on end user searching in libraries. In Williams, M. E., and Hogan, T. H., eds. *National online meeting proceedings—1986.* Medford, N.J.: Learned Information, 347–52.

Peters, T. J. 1988. *Thriving on chaos: Handbook for a management revolution.* Perennial Library Edition. New York: Harper & Row.

———, and Austin, N. 1985. *A passion for excellence; The leadership difference.* New York: Warner Books.

Peters, T. J., and Waterman, R. H., Jr. 1982. *In search of excellence.* New York: Warner Books.

Pratt, A. D. 1984. Microcomputers in libraries. *Annual Review of Information Science and Technology* 19: 248.

Public Library Data Service. 1989. *Statistical report 89.* Chicago: Public Library Association, American Library Association.

Rosch, W. L. 1988. Low-end networks fit work groups best. *Connectivity* 5 (June 21): 21–22.

Rosenburg, P. 1985. *Costfinding for public libraries; A manager's handbook.* Chicago: American Library Association.

Saffady, W. 1987. The Macintosh as a library workstation: A report on available hardware and software. *Library Technology Reports* 23 (January–February): 5–196.

Stallings, W. 1985. *Computer communications: Architecture, protocols and standards.* Washington, D.C.: IEEE Computer Society Press.
———. 1987. *Local networks.* 2nd ed. New York: Macmillan.
Stanek, D. J. 1986. Videotapes, computer programs, and the library. *Information Technology and Libraries* (March): 42–54.
Steffen, S. S. 1987. Living with and managing change: A case study of the Schaffner Library. *Illinois Libraries* (February): 126–29.
Tannenbaum, A. S. 1981a. *Computer networks.* Englewood Cliffs, N.J.: Prentice-Hall.
———. 1981b. Network Protocols. *Computing surveys.* 13 (December): 453–89.
Toong, H. D., and Gupta, A. 1982. Personal computers. *Scientific American* 247 (6): 86–107.
Valauskas, E. J. 1988. The NeXT computer system: The next library workstation? *Library Workstation and PC Report* 5 (December): 9–11.
———. 1989. NeXT and the library workstation. *OCLC Micro* 5 (February): 12–14.
Vandergrift, K. E. 1988. Hypermedia: Breaking the tyranny of the text. *School Library Journal* 35 (November): 30–35.
Wallace, D. P., and Giglierano, J. 1989. Microcomputers in libraries. *Library Trends* 37 (Winter): 282–301.
The workstation revolution. *Scientific American* 260 (5): w1–w9.
Zimmerman, H. 1980. OSI Reference Model—The ISO model of architecture for open systems interconnection. *IEEE Transactions on Communication* 28 (April): 425–32.

I N D E X

Acquisition files
  linking with catalog files, 87
Acquisitions, 86
  financial aspects, 88
  serials control, 88
  spreadsheet use, 87
American Society of Safety Engineers
  types of VDT tasks, 102

Bad posture
  possible medical problems, 106
Bar-codes
  circulation use, 93
Baseband systems, 125
Bibliography, 145
Bibliophile
  Library Corporation, 90
Broadband systems, 124
BUS network design, 117

Cables
  for local area networks, 126
Catalog card production programs, 92
Cataloger's workstations
  definition, 89
Cataloging during acquisitions, 88
CCITT X.25 interface standard, 123
CD-ROM
  acquisitions, 87
  advantages, 86
  use in technical services, 85
CD-ROM public use
  further reading, 82
CD-ROM reference sources and online
  services, 76
CD-ROM reference tools
  applications software problems, 75
Change
  management of, 25
  positive effects, 29
  potential reactions illustration, 27
  resistance to, 27
Circulation systems
  bar-code-based, 92
  database creation, 95

inventory-control problem, 92
  materials preparation, 95
  patron access, 96
  patron database, 96
  steps in automating, 94
  testing the system, 96
  vendor list, 94
  weeding prior to bar-coding, 94
CLSI workstation, 90
Computers
  library staff reactions, 28
Computers as consumables, 21
Connectivity issues, 72
Contention access systems
  carrier-sense multiple access (CSMA),
    119
CONTU and copyright law, 72
Copyright issues
  law, 72
  issues for librarians, 73
Copyright Law
  ease of infringement, 18
Cost-benefit analysis
  local area networks and workstations,
    49
Costs of computers
  illustration, 7
Creation of "good associates," 31

Decision-Information Systems
  further reading, 66
Dedicated communication lines
  advantages, 123
Desktop publishing
  counting the costs, 64
  in library public relations, 64
Digital dataphone service, 124
Disk storage capacity
  librarian's workstation, 19
Document delivery services
  dealing with public demand, 79
Documenting decision process, 43
Dot matrix characters
  illustration, 103
DVORAK keyboard design, 109

Electronic mail, 58
Ergonomics
  in library operations, 101
Error checking
  in local area networks, 120

FAX machines
  interlibrary-loan use, 77
  paying the costs, 80
Fee or free questions
  further reading, 81
  online and CD-ROM services, 79
Fiber-optic cables for LANS
  advantages, 126
File servers
  STAR networks, 116
Form responses
  advantages, 54
Forms for routine communications, 53
Frequency-division multiplexing, 120
Full-text retrieval services
  advantages for the public, 76

Gateways, 122
Geac Corporation
  WYSE workstations, 90
Grammar- and style-checking programs
  list, 56
Graphic capabilities
  librarian's workstation, 17
  public access workstations, 70
Growth problems in LANS
  strategies for handling, 42

H. W. Wilson Reference CDs, 75
Hacking and virus problems, 69
Hard disk drive failures, 19
Hard disk drives, 6
  menu programs, 6–7
Human factors design
  in workstations, 107
Human positions
  effect of various positions, 105
Hypercard
  capabilities, 18
Hypertext
  further reading, 24

Incompatibility of computers, 5
Indexing software
  local applications, 81
Information Society
  library's potential role, 45
Institute of Electrical and Electronic
    Engineers
  802 Committee, 121

Instructing the public
  further reading, 82
Interlibrary loan activities, 77
Interlibrary Loan Micro Enhancer
  OCLC, 91
ISBN
  use in circulation systems, 95
Island culture concept, 34

Keyboard design, 108

LaserGuide
  General Research Corporation, 91
LePac CD-ROM catalog
  Brodart, 91
Librarian's workstation
  capabilities, 15
  differences from scholar workstation, 15
Librarians' guidelines for LANS, 127
Library computer use
  total staff involvement, 33
Library Corporation's Bibliophile, 90
Library correspondence
  management analysis of, 50
Library information processing needs
  analysis, 21
Library local area networks
  long-term process, 34
Library management
  access to network statistics, 50
  workstation applications, 49
Library manager's workstation
  characteristics, 52
  primary purpose, 52
Library networks
  further reading, 132
Library workstations
  definition, 85
  shared uses, 51
  use analysis, 51
Linked Systems Project
  use of OSI model, 121
Local area network planning
  questions to ask, 38
Local area networks
  advantages, 9
  baseband systems, 125
  broadband systems, 124
  cable selection, 126, 128
  component tools, 10
  considerations in starting, 22
  contrasted with telecommunications
      systems, 10
  curve of nonsatisfaction, 34
  data protection, 44

documenting process, 43
growth problems, 42
guidelines for librarians, 127
impact on future library management, 37
low-cost options, 11, 13
manufacturers (list), 139
network administrator's responsibilities, 39
new opportunities for libraries, 35
organizational effects illustration, 29
potential problems, 20
protocols, 11
security considerations, 41
selecting staff, 37
standards, 114, 119
training needs assessment, 43
Local public-access databases, 80
Low-cost LANS, 136
Low-cost networks
advantages, 12

M300 workstation series, 90
Macintosh computer
advantages for library applications, 17
Mail-merge programs
example, 55
Managing change
further reading, 47
Managing people during change
essential steps, 30
MARC records, 89
use in circulation systems, 95
Maverick computing, 43
overcoming, 23
MICROCON
OCLC, 92
Mobile data radio systems
use and limitations, 124
Modems
script programs, 5
speed, 5
Monitoring workflow
problems, 37
Multiplexing techniques, 120

Network administrator
responsibilities, 38–39
Network Advisory Committee
Library of Congress, 121
NeXT computer
features, 14
Null modems
connections illustrated, 115
defined, 6

Object-oriented processors, 18
OCLC
workstations development, 90
OCLC CJK350 System, 91
Office arrangement
human factors effects, 110
Online and CD-ROM reference services
paying for services, 79
Online catalog systems
as local area networks, 63
library manager's analysis, 63
Online catalogs
CD-ROM versions, 91
Online Computer Library Center (OCLC), 4
Online public access catalogs
as reference workstations, 80
training the public, 80
Online reference services
front-end software protocols, 76
public expectations, 76
Online services
advantages and disadvantages, 86
Online systems
use of personal computers, 4
Open Systems Interconnection Reference Model
further reading, 129
illustration, 122
OSI 7498, 120
Operating speed
librarian's workstation, 19

Pace of change, 26
Packet switching
contention access schemes, 119
Packets
on local area networks, 118
Patrons' records
confidentiality, 77
Peer-to-peer networks
table of characteristics, 136
Peripheral sharing devices
switching systems, 11
Personal computers
compared with typewriters, 101
early library uses, 3
incompatability, 20
simple interconnections, 114
Planning process
staff inclusion in, 28
Plasma display devices
list, 74
Point-to-point connections
costs, 115

Printers
    location, 69
Printing capabilities
    librarian's workstation, 19
Psychological denial systems, 32
Public-access workstations
    analysis of software needs, 78
    as reference resources, 75
    assigning management responsibilities, 68
    demands on staff and equipment, 73
    equipment selection, 70
    establishing goals, 67
    graphic capabilities, 70
    protecting patron confidentiality, 77
    security, 69
    site selection and layout, 68
    software collection development, 78
    software selection, 72, 83
    specific issues, 67
    use of equipment policies, 74
Public packet networks, 123

QWERTY keyboard design, 109

Readability and legibility tasks
    differences, 102
Repeaters
    use in local area networks, 126
Retrospective conversion
    conversion options, 97
    establishing priority areas, 97
    multiple database problem, 97
    vendor quality control, 98
RING networks, 116–118
RLN workstation, 90
Routine communications
    analysis, 53

Scanning devices
    use in desktop publishing, 64
Scholar workstations, 14
    capabilities, 71
Security systems
    local area networks, 41
Serial ports
    RS232 connections, 115
Serials
    acquisition and control, 88
Serials costs
    longitudinal studies, 88
Serials records
    retrospective conversion, 89
Slotted-ring concept, 118
Software for public use
    collection development, 78
    selection, 72, 83

Software use by public
    need for policy, 73
Spell-checking programs, 56
Spreadsheet programs
    applications in planning, budgeting,
        evaluation, 59
    illustrations, 60, 62
    what-if applications, 61
    further reading, 65
Staff reactions to computers, 28
Stand-alone computer systems, 4
Standards
    further reading, 129
STAR network illustrated, 116

Technical services
    further reading, 98
    online or local, 85
Technical services workstations
    OCLC guides, 91
Technological change
    impact on people, 25
Technological developments
    accelerating change, 46
Technology
    fear of, 26
    humane policies about use, 35
    impact on library's way of doing
        business, 26
    views of, 26
Text display
    monitors, 15
Time-division multiplexing, 120
Token ring systems
    advantages, 118
Training in technological applications
    alternatives, 32
TREE network design, 117

VDT devices
    angle of viewing, 104
    contrast and color, 102
    display devices, 101
    factors affecting display, 102
    flicker, 102
    further reading, 113
    glare problems, 104
    image refreshing, 103
    office lighting, 105

Weeding collections
    prior to automation, 94
What-you-see-is-what-you-get programs,
    57
Wide Area Networks, 122
Word processing applications, 53

Word processing programs
  CD-ROM enhancements, 57
  file and format transfer programs, 58
  policies needed, 57
  search capabilities, 55
Work design dimensions
  human factors, 30
Workplace attitudes, 32
Workstation ergonomics
  further reading, 112
Workstation management applications, 49
Workstation revolution, 30
Workstations
  acquisitions, 87
  cataloging functions, 89
  circulation systems, 92
  electrical requirements, 70
  first stage of development, 8
  human factors design recommendations,
    107

human factors design illustrated, 108
keyboard design, 108
placement in office settings, 110
producers (list), 133
protocols and interconnections, 114
second stage of development, 8
site and layout, 68
specific posture problems, 106
standards, 114
technical services uses, 85
third stage of development (LANS), 9
wiring problems, 111
WYSE workstations
  OCLC adoption, 90

X.25 interface standard
  CCITT, 123

Z39.50 standard, 121

Kieth C. Wright is a professor in the Department of Library and Information Studies at the University of North Carolina at Greensboro, where he teaches courses in library automation, online retrieval, and electronic information systems for libraries. He holds an MLS and DLS in Computer Analysis from Columbia University. Wright is the author of several books and articles on library services for the disabled, including *The Library Manager's Guide to Serving and Employing Disabled Persons* (McFarland, 1990).